The
Best
of
Costume Jewelry

Nancy Schiffer
Photography by Tim Scott

Schiffer Publishing Ltd

Acknowledgements

Wonderful collections of jewelry have been viewed over the years, a process which has significantly contributed to the overall understanding of trends which are presented here. We appreciate each person's time and shared enthusiasm, for that has kept the search for varied examples alive.

We especially thank Veronica Manussis of Cobra and Bellamy, London; David Lancaster of Christie's South Kensington; Lucia Lambert of Bel Arte, Burlington Arcade, London; and Ian Harris of N. Bloom & Sons, London, all of whom made their outstanding collections of jewelry available to us.

We thank particularly the staff and Sonny and Lawrence Feldman of Fior, London, who were the inspiration, for they opened their trove for us to see, added personal remarks about the manufacturers, and helped make this project so enjoyable.

I thank Tim Scott for his help in organizing the material. His talent behind the camera will be further appreciated by all who view his photographs.

Title page:
Necklace of amethyst-colored European glass beads, pearls and colored stones set in a fringe design, French origin, probably late 1940s.

Opposite:
Earrings of wired metal and colored glass beads and pearls, and bearing a metal tag marked Givenchy, 1950s, courtesy of Bel Arte, London.

Copyright © 1990 by Nancy Schiffer.
Library of Congress Catalog Number: 89-64088.

Printed in the United States of America.
ISBN: 0-88740-223-2

Published by Schiffer Publishing, Ltd.
1469 Morstein Road
West Chester, Pennsylvania 19380
Please write for a free catalog.
This book may be purchased from the publisher.
Please include $2.00 postage.
Try your bookstore first.

Contents

Necklace, brooch, and pair of earrings
constructed with translucent enamel, wire,
and rhinestones mixed with pearls, 1950s,
Gripoix, Courtesy of Cobra and Bellamy,
London.

Preface

The "Best" is hard to define, for it necessarily judges design and craftsmanship to eliminate many jewelry pieces that are truly wonderful. There are so many costume jewelry firms that have made excellent pieces but could not be included because of space. Once familiar with the quality presented here, each reader will be able to identify those pieces themselves, for they stand apart.

The jewelry shown on the following pages was selected from several of the "best" collections known. Much of it is in the Fior collection in London, unless otherwise noted. Comprising thousands of pieces, this special collection from many regions of the world represents some of the finest costume jewelry dating back to the 1920s and forward to current retail stock. The history of this specialized retail firm is presented in Lawrence Feldman's Introduction to this book. While this is but one firm's story, it may be expanded to represent the whole of the industry, for the popular growth of costume jewelry as a field of general interest internationally roughly corresponds with the time period that the Fior firm was growing in London.

Parallels can be made with Fior and other shops in other cities. As London (and Paris, Rome, Geneva, Munich, Amsterdam, Tehran, Tel Aviv, Hong Kong, New York, Los Angeles, Tokyo...) grew more cosmopolitan, it became no longer unusual to see people in foreign dress shopping for luxuries of personal apparel.

Higher standards of living worldwide enabled long distance travel to be commonplace. With the spread of an international clientele came the dissemination of a more general interest in fine costume jewelry. And so this book begins to document the best jewelry which has become precious to its owners over time, even if it was not thought of as precious when it was first acquired.

The illustrations are grouped by their manufacturers, where know, and chronologically by the high point of each company. Therefore, when a company progressed through several decades, the jewelry by that firm will be found together, related in its design concepts, rather than in a strict chronological sequence. As we study the jewelry, it becomes more interesting to see how the designs evolved from each designer/manufacturer before we realize that a time sequence is also in play. And thereby the related jewelry can be viewed in close proximity.

As the international art market keeps changing through time, different cities have risen to take leadership roles providing the origins, and consumers, of popular taste. In the twentieth century the shifts in this leadership have been swift and worldwide, including Moscow, Berlin, Vienna, Paris, London, New York, Los Angeles, and Tokyo.

The general popularity of costume jewelry steadily grew during the middle of the twentieth century. World events conspired to make London one of the centers of world fashion taste by the 1960s, and people in America and the Middle East some of the most enthusiastic consumers. Yet distribution of the goods was worldwide, touching markets in every small town and big city through advertising on radio and television, and in newspaper chains which span the globe. As twentieth century taste changed more rapidly and completely than ever before, an atmosphere was created where everyone—each individual—could find their own preferred style among the plethora of types available.

Two brooches and two pairs of earrings set with colored cabochon stones, rhinestones and pearls, Gripoix, 1950s, Courtesy of Cobra and Bellamy, London.

Introduction

by Lawrence Feldman

While clothing is a necessity, personal adornment is an expression of individual personality. Wearing jewelry is not so much a vanity as a natural instinct.

The great designs of the major jewelry houses have been reinterpreted in materials from noble to base metals, and from valuable gem stones to colored glass. The precious jewelry has been emulated in materials that most every woman can afford.

This group of costume jewelry follows in design traditional European styles. It is hand finished and 18kt. gold plated. Some of the 30-year-old pieces occasionally have been replated and reset to refresh their original appearance.

The popular use of costume jewelry has always been a very Anglo-American phenomenon. It was in the USA that this remarkable industry blossomed into the sophisticated and lucrative industry which it now is.

Emanating mainly from New York and Providence, Rhode Island, countless manufacturers were involved in producing enormous quantities of costume jewelry for the home market. What is remarkable is that like the major couture houses, these manufacturers produced two collections each year, a truly formidable task.

While American and English women have worn costume jewelry regularly for a generation, only in the last few years has the average European woman accepted that costume jewelry is a legitimate fashion accessory. No longer does the average French, Italian, or central European woman shun them. Previously, although they may have dressed in perfect taste, with carefully chosen accessories, unless they were very wealthy, the jewelry they wore was inordinately dull and boring. The great couture houses of France and Italy marketed their own "designer" jewelry, but these pieces were produced in tiny quantities for a wealthy and sophisticated clientele.

Silver wings pin by Trifari; blue and clear stone choker by Boucher; sunburst pin by Kramer; two gold and silver pins with rhinestones by Trifari, 1960s.

I have already mentioned that wearing costume jewelry is predominantly an Anglo-American phenomenon. I believe that this is largely due to the "big store" mentality and purchasing patterns of the U.K. and U.S.A.

In the last few years an increasing number of manufacturers have come into the market, and many of the major fashion houses now have their own costume jewelry business. While some of these new manufacturers market good quality merchandise, there is unfortunately a plethora of badly made, overpriced, so-called "designer" jewelry which has done much harm to the so-recently-gained good reputation of the industry.

When a beautifully-made piece of antique costume jewelry is compared to the best that is made today, there is remarkably little difference (in quality). This means perhaps that the perfection of the art was reached early in its career, and that unlike so many other industries, advances in manufacturing techniques and materials are not readily apparent. This must be a complement to those who were producing forty to fifty years ago, and likewise to those few top manufacturers who still produce jewelry to the same high standards.

A Retail History

Building upon a family tradition, Sonny Feldman (b.1910) formed the firm of Feldman & Inwald in the East End of London around 1933. His father had opened a jewelry business in London in 1892, but Sonny had no interest in joining his father in the business which, to his youthful thinking, had no glamour, little fashion, catered mainly to older people, and moved at a snail's pace. He was trained in the real jewelry business, and that training was to manifest itself later.

The Feldman & Inwald (Inwald was a silent partner) shop was situated on Whitechapel Road which, prior to World War II was a fine, wide avenue in the East End of London. This area was predominantly a Jewish neighborhood where

Five pins made in the late 1960s: rhinestone comet design by Kramer of New York; bowknot of gold-plated metal and rhinestones by Castlecliff; pearl and gold circle pin by Trifari; topaz and diamond pin; and gold leaf pin with silver and rhinestone group in center.

many people had come to live following their arrival in England to escape pogroms in Eastern Europe. By the 1930s, second- and third-generation families were spreading into other areas of London and its suburbs and, of course, the fine shops on Whitechapel Road attracted a good non-local clientele as well.

Feldman & Inwald sold a range of fashion accessories including day and evening handbags, belts, wallets, gloves, and popular jewelry. Much of the then-in-vogue Art Deco jewelry was sold, reaching its zenith of popularity in the 1930s. By then, Sonny Feldman was importing and selling jewelry by Trifari of the U.S.A. and Henkel & Grosse of Germany. In fact, these manufacturers were the first suppliers of costume jewelry in England. Jewelry was also imported from France which had, at that time, an important and influential place in the fashion market.

Progress in this thriving business was halted by the second World War. Mr. Feldman had joined the service early in the war, and ultimately the lack of personal supervision and virtually no new merchandise all but destroyed the firm.

The East End of London was particularly badly damaged during the war, leaving Whitechapel Road a rather sad place. Badly scarred, its attraction was

---

Necklace and two pins of French origin, 1940s, utilizing brass and colored glass beads.

lost forever. These were difficult days. Manufacturing in England had been devastated and raw materials were almost impossible to obtain. Furthermore, free importation was banned and exchange controls were strictly enforced. However, Mr. Feldman was fortunate in having limited government-issued import licenses which were given only to those who had previously imported goods. These meagre licenses were based on turnover, but at least some importation was permitted. He used his good fortune to secure goods from Germany, Italy, France, and the U.S.A.

Necklace from the 1940s made in two strands of small prong-set rhinestones and colored glass beads as fringe, unmarked.

As the country very slowly recovered, money gradually became more available than goods and Feldman & Inwald's business continued as they offered glamorous accessories to a very grey, deprived London clientele.

When an opportunity arose for a relocation near Bond Street in the fashionable Mayfair section of London, Feldman lost no time in securing it. Consistent with evolving merchandising methods, he also decided that a shorter name for the new business would be advantageous if it were to be an avant-garde shop for fine fashion accessories. After deciding that the initial letters of Feldman & Inwald would be retained, a short list of possible words was drawn up which included "fior"—the Italian word for flower—and this was chosen for the new firm.

In September, 1950, a brand new shop called Fior was opened at Nos. 3-5 Burlington Gardens. This is a charming little street off Old Bond Street in the heart of London which houses the northern end of the Burlington Arcade and the back of the Royal Academy. Fior faced both of these. For all its basis in tradition, Fior was not an ordinary shop. Instead, it had been designed as an exciting statement of the avant-garde by the brilliant architect Werner Heumann, who now resides in California. The shop became a talking point of London and attracted architects and retailers from all over the world.

The Visitor's Book of 1950-52 shows that customers included respected members of London society as well as international film and television celebrities such as British actresses Sylvia Sims, Joan Collins, Diana Dors,

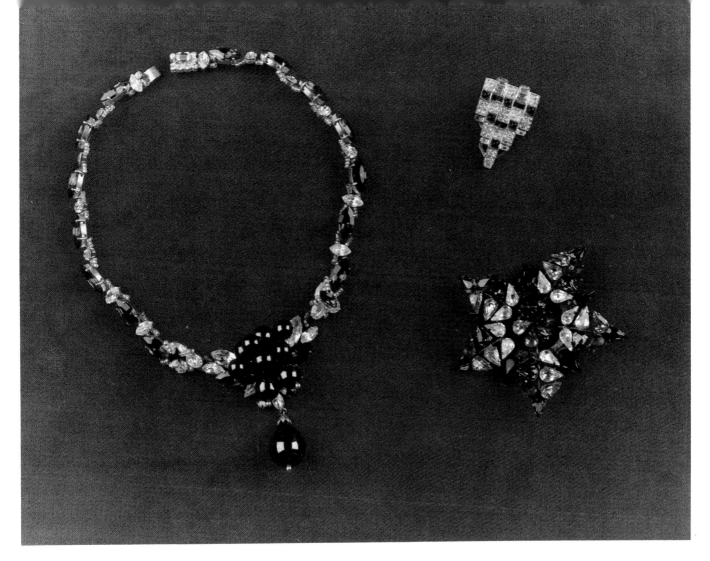

and Kay Kendall. Lucille Ball, James Stewart, and Pier Angeli were early customers. Among clients from the high society were Princess Alexandra of Kent and other members of the Royal Family.

Fior regularly supplied jewelry and accessories to companies of the British film industry such as Pinewood, Elstree, and others.

In 1956, Fior was granted a Royal Warrant by Prince Bernard of the Netherlands, and was thereby the first costume jeweler to receive such an honor. As the firm continued to grow, it attracted the next generation for Sonny's sons, Michael and Lawrence, who joined the business in 1957 and 1959 respectively. Michael Feldman introduced quality leather goods and built this into

Necklace, clip, and pin of French origin from the 1940s. An assortment of colored and clear stones have been cleverly combined in these pieces to create jewelry of classic good taste which was saleable in a conservative market.

an important part of the Fior business. In 1966 he won and still controls the Celine franchise at the Brompton Road shop. Lawrence had an affinity for jewelry and still continues to direct this part of the firm. The eldest brother, Peter, a chartered accountant, joined Fior in 1973 and runs the administrative duties.

During the 1960s London was becoming a more highly fashionable city with international attention focusing on evolving trends. It began to attract the new elite customers as more quality shops and hotels were opened. In response, the Fior personnel reacted quickly to evolving fashion trends and cultivated their more numerous clientele.

In 1962 Lawrence Feldman spent six months at the jewelry manufacturing factory of the Grosse Jewels company in Pforzheim, Germany, refining his knowledge of jewelry design, manufacturing techniques, and goldsmithing.

About this time American actress Elizabeth Taylor commissioned Fior to produce for security reasons, an exact replica in glass stones of one of her emerald-set pieces.

In 1968 a new shop was opened around the corner in Bond Street. It was

architecturally related to the existing Burlington Gardens shop. Shortly thereafter the landlords of the Burlington Gardens shop decided to redevelop that site and demolish the existing building including the Fior shop.

The Feldmans soon located a new site for their business on Brompton Road, Knightsbridge, just a few doors from Harrod's store. This was a commercial center of already-proven importance to London's art and luxury business. With shops now in two of the most important retail streets in London, Fior's future grew into a major force in the accessories business.

During the decade of the 1970s, London's importance in the fashion and financial circles strengthened, and the numerous fashion changes demanded

---

Necklace and two pairs of earrings made from silver and tiny rhinestones, French origin, 1940s.

access to a wide choice of accessories and jewels. Soon costume jewelry became important to the mass market for women of all countries, young and older. Before long the potential for this market was recognized by many of the major international fashion houses who introduced their own lines of costume jewelry.

Fior faced the challenge of widespread competition by developing their own interpretations of the jewelry collections of the great international jewelers. Fior even offered wristwatches under the Fior name.

In 1985 curators from the Victoria and Albert Museum in London, recognizing the wide popular interest in costume jewelry, approached Fior to stage an exhibition of fine costume jewelry from the twentieth century. Drawing from its historical collection, Fior provided stunning material to this first public showing. Attendance at the exhibition surpassed all expectations; supplies of the specially printed museum leaflet describing the exhibition were exhausted by the end of the first day. Subsequently, Fior has donated several important pieces of its jewelry to the museum's permanent collection.

The popularity of jewelry in general, and fine costume jewelry in particular, was stimulated by the sale in Geneva in 1987 of the Duchess of Windsor's jewels through Sotheby's auction house. The event received massive publicity and the jewels fetched huge sums of money (much of it given to a favorite charity of the Duchess's choosing). With that inspiration, people from all levels of society aspired to have their own beautiful jewelry.

Successful and highly glamorous television programs such as "Dallas" and "Dynasty" have also influenced the jewelry field, dictating a more extravagant and aggressive style of dressing.

The Fior collection grows steadily through the years as selected pieces are removed from the shop inventory regularly to be kept for posterity. Almost every facet of costume jewelry is represented—from full sets to individual pieces of special design. The collection is remarkable in that it is in pristine condition, since the jewelry has not been worn. It is hoped that the collection can be seen and used by people who are interested in its special characteristics.

Necklace and flower pin from the late nineteenth century, probably English, with clear stones. The pair of clips were made by Trifari in the late 1940s in the style of their Victorian predecessors. Courtesy of N. Bloom & Son, London.

1940s

The world of fashion was closing down at the beginning of the decade as political events threw the world into a time of war. Rations were imposed on European populations from 1941, and metals formerly used in the costume jewelry manufacturing process were requisitioned for military purposes. In America, sterling silver was still available for jewelry even when rhodium and pot metals were scarce. Copper and brass were utilized for costume jewelry to a great extent giving rise to interesting chain designs. When it became impossible for American manufacturers to obtain fresh supplies of glass beads and fine quality rhinestones from their origins in Eastern Europe, old reserves were used from former years and combinations of materials not previously used together were made. Therefore, some of the jewelry from this period has small stones, and multicolored combinations mixed with metal links and metal parts.

When the Second World War finally was over in 1945, the designs of costume jewelry continued to be conservative, in keeping with the moods of the customers who needed to maintain restrained appearances. But women wanted to maintain their femininity, too, and supported the accessories market in gradually increasing numbers as their prosperity improved. The young House of Dior caused a sensation in fashion circles in 1947 when it showed their "New Look" collection of dresses with full and longer skirts, curved shoulder lines and accessories including jewelry.

The costume jewelry of the 1940s reflects the swinging moods of the people as the examples which follow demonstrate.

Three necklaces of prong-set iridescent stones set in brass and with glass beads as fringe, 1940s. The glass, which reflects a prism of colored light, is sometimes called Aurora Borealis.

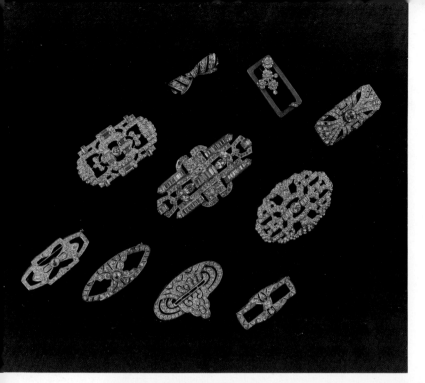

Opposite:
Six double clips of French origin made from sterling silver and clear and colored rhinestones in the 1940s.

Group of ten pins with small, clear rhinestones made in the 1930s and 1940s.

Group of jewelry spanning three decades yet harmonious in style and materials. The clip with turquoise and coral colored stones dates from the 1930s. The bracelet and double clip marked Nymph are French from the 1940s. The 1950s necklace was made by D'Orlan of Canada.

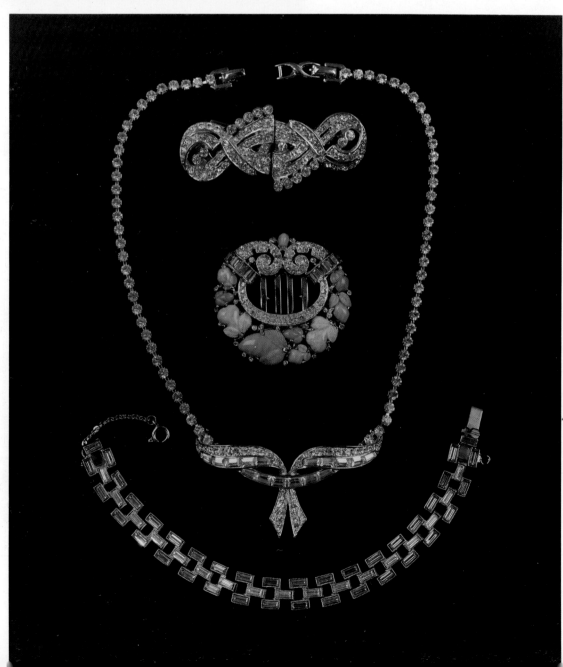

Opposite:
Single clips of small clear
rhinestones and colored glass in
designs which by the 1940s
when these were made were
classic.

Four pins and five pairs of
earrings from the 1940s made
from silver and pot metal and
small clear and colored
rhinestones and pearls.

Three pins and three pairs of
clips from the 1940s made with
gold washed metal and clear
rhinestones.

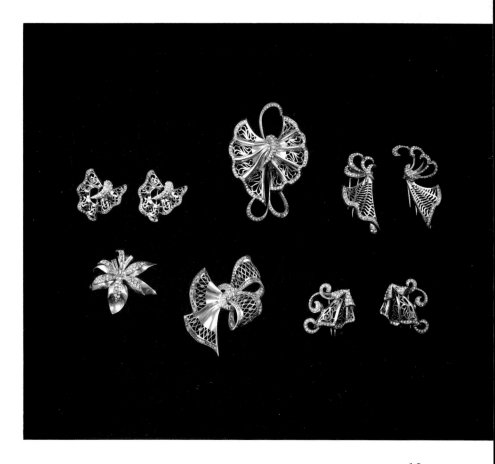

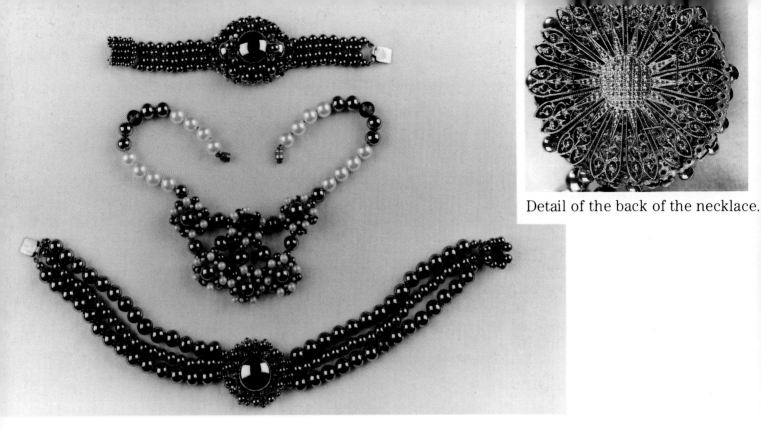

Detail of the back of the necklace.

Two French necklaces and one bracelet, all marked M. B. from the late 1940s. The use of colored glass beads from Central Europe was curtailed for a time, but old stocks were used to create new designs. The medallions are wired to ornate cast plates.

Glass bead necklace of assorted colors and graduated sizes from the 1940s shown with a pair of earrings of cast and plated metal and cabochon glass stones made in the mid-1950s by Jomaz. The continuity of design between these two forms is apparent even when their origins are distant.

Brass necklace and bracelet set of interesting ovoid links and a white enamel-on-brass linked necklace from the 1940s.

Two necklaces of brass and one of colored stones set as flower heads, 1940s.

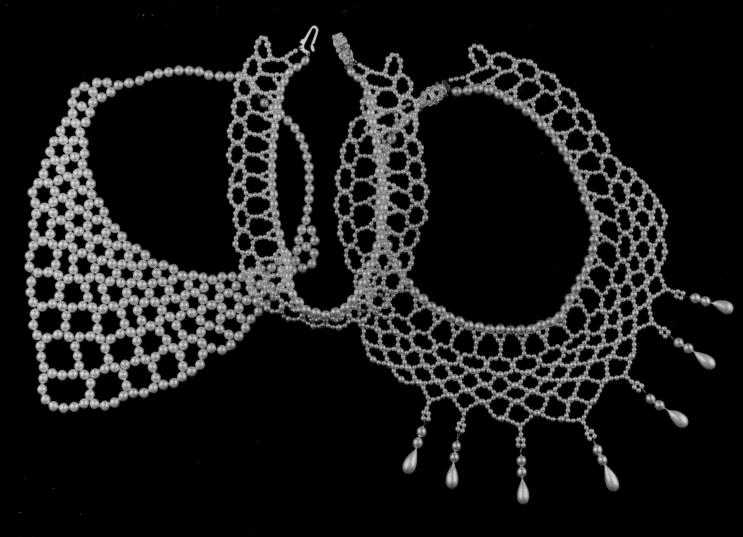

Opposite:
Three pearl lace necklaces, the ones to the left and center are English while the one to the right is French.

Pearl choker and bracelet set with rhinestone-set clasps made circa 1946.

French brass necklace with rhinestones, and copper and brass choker of chain mail from the 1940s shown with a pair of gold plated German earrings.

Boucher

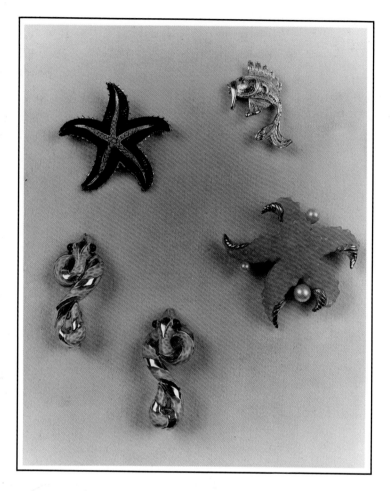

Marcel Boucher, one of the greatest names in the costume jewelry field, designed gem-set jewelry for Cartier in New York after his arrival in America from France in 1925. His talent extended to many forms of jewelry design and he made his own pieces under his own signature in the early 1940s. Costume jewelry was among his production, and it was of the highest quality technically. Sandra Boucher, Marcel's wife and also a talented designer, joined the Boucher firm in 1960 and carried on the company after Marcel's death in 1965. The firm continued to produce fine quality costume jewelry until 1970.

Jewelry of an aquatic theme: black starfish and sterling silver fish unmarked, green starfish by Boucher, green serpent earrings by Trifari.

Three figural pins by Boucher which include interesting patterned stones and pearls.

Distinguished by superb design and quality, his production reached its zenith in the 1950s and 1960s. His pieces reflect all that was best in real jewelry design in this period. A unique specialty was his use of baguettes, both straight and tapered, which was never equalled before or since by any other manufacturer. He used stones of superb color and quality, and chain and hand finishes such as "Florentine" engraving, brilliantly. Almost everything by Boucher is worth collecting; they are scarce and valuable. Boucher signed all his pieces together with his own reference number.

Bracelet and three pins of exquisite quality and combination of materials by Boucher.

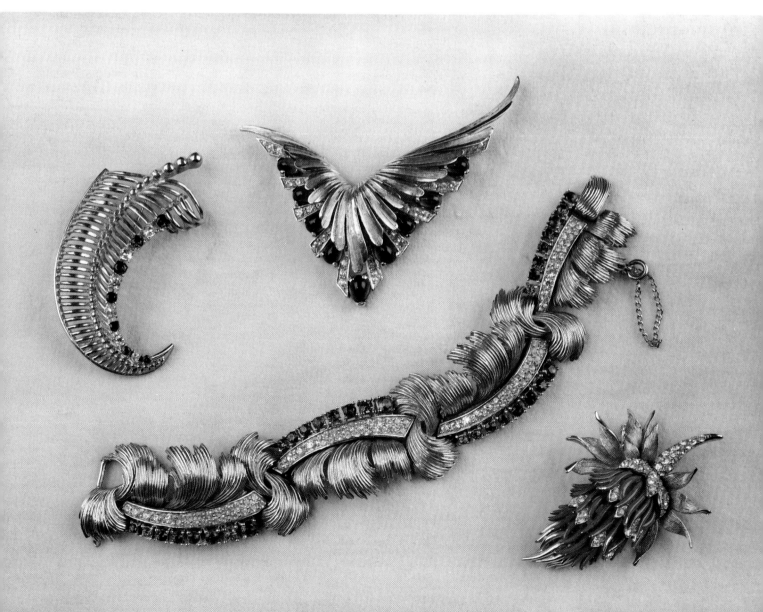

Necklace, bracelet, and pair of earrings by Boucher with green cabochons clustered with clear rhinestones. Courtesy of Cobra and Bellamy, London.

Bowknot pin of colored enamel and green cabochon surrounded by rhinestones made by Boucher, and a small twisted oval enameled pin by Ciner.

26

Two pins and a pair of earrings of colored glass and rhinestones in a leaf design by Boucher.

Earrings by Boucher of gilded metal and blue cabochons similar to the bracelet shown at the bottom of page 28, and three bracelets of similar character but unsigned.

Deep relief Buddah pin by Boucher shown with a cameo set in enameled frame by Jomaz.

Necklace of rhinestone-studded metal links and pin with three-dimensional bowknot design by Boucher.

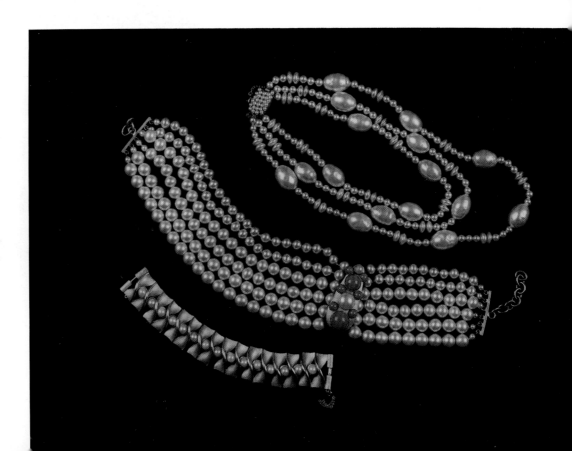

Pendant necklace, link bracelet, pin and
earrings set (1959), paisley leaf pin (1959)
and ivory flower pin, all by Boucher.

Opposite:
Pearl jewelry was popular and exotic in the
1940s and many costume jewelry designers
made their own designs to show off the luster
of the pearls. The three-strand necklace has
pearls of unusual shapes and is unmarked.
The six-strand necklace with coral-colored
stones in a plaque is from Italy. The bracelet
with metal bow links was made by Boucher.

Six pins of various gold-plated designs by
Boucher.

Necklace of blue and clear stones, and a pin
and pair of earrings of gilded metal, red
cabochons and rhinestones by Boucher.
Courtesy of Cobra and Bellamy, London.

Gilt necklace with colored stones and two brooches (the leaf design is the earlier one) by Boucher. Courtesy of Cobra and Bellamy, London.

Blue and clear bowknot pin, 1958; crescent earrings, 1955; disc earrings, 1955; leaf-shaped pin with clear stones, 1957, all by Boucher.

Two pairs of earrings, circa 1955, chain bracelet with compass charm inscribed "Do Not Lose Your Bearing," link bracelet set with pearl and turquoise stones, enameled pineapple pin, and gilded flower head pin, all by Boucher.

Coro

Early in the 1900s, partners Mr. Cohn and Gerald Rosenberger began Coro to bring reasonably priced jewelry "to the people." By the late 1920s their manufacturing was done in Providence, Rhode Island, and in the 1940s they began the Corocraft line. Characterized by the most current fashion, a piece of "Coro" was affordable to every woman of all ages, including teenagers.

Later, their best jewelry was presented in their Vendome line. For Vendome they produced some excellent, witty designs which were well made and superb value at the time. Standouts included ranges of double pins incorporating motifs such as animals.

An important manufacturing base was set up in England to supply the British, European and Commonwealth markets, using many American designs. Increasingly, British designs were created for the new markets, reflecting very often a different approach to the non-U.S. market. The president of Coro U.K. was Fred Plato, who rose from office boy to head the firm. There was also a Coro of Canada.

After Gerald Rosenberger and Fred Plato retired, the company ceased production in the 1970s. Their use of colored and irridescent stones in combination was unparalleled, and their designs were delicate. Their cast pieces were always signed but those that were not signed included soldered pressings, bead necklaces and other novelties.

Pair of earrings and pendant/pin, Vendome by Coro.

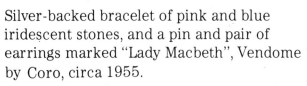

Necklace and two butterfly-shaped pins set with multi-colored stones, Vendome by Coro

Silver-backed bracelet of pink and blue iridescent stones, and a pin and pair of earrings marked "Lady Macbeth", Vendome by Coro, circa 1955.

Matching set of necklace, bracelet, and
earrings by Coro featuring pearls and floral
clusters, mid-1950s.

Haskell

Miriam Haskell designed and sold fashionable, high quality costume jewelry in New York from 1924 through the 1950s, and the company, under new management, continues today. Distinctive were her use of tiny seed pearls in clusters and her soft-toned gilding which emulated ancient granulation techniques. The result was usually a shimmering and provocative creation.

Opposite:
Necklace bearing Miriam Haskell's oval tag at the closure and a dramatic and bold combination of various pearls, leaf medallions and chains. Courtesy of Bel Arte, London.

Necklace of two strands of pearls with gold spacers and pendant floral cluster, and a pair of drop earrings by Miriam Haskell. Courtesy of Bel Arte, London.

Necklace of graduated pearls and pendant
cluster by Miriam Haskell. Courtesy of Bel
Arte, London.

Opposite:
Two-strand pearl necklace with elaborate
fringe and medallion catch/pendant by
Miriam Haskell. Courtesy of Bel Arte, London.

Matching fringe necklace and pair of drop
earrings by Miriam Haskell. Courtesy of Bel
Arte, London.

Three-strand necklace of Baroque pearls by
Miriam Haskell. Courtesy of Bel Arte, London.

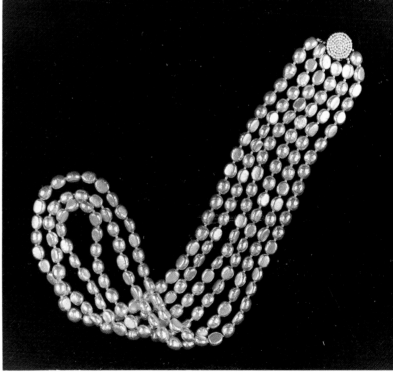

Opposite:
Twisted chain and floral cluster necklace of dynamic character by Miriam Haskell. Courtesy of Bel Arte, London.

Two-strand Baroque pearl necklace with a cluster and pearl catch/pendant by Miriam Haskell. Courtesy of Bel Arte, London.

Blue glass bead pendant necklace and pair of earrings by Miriam Haskell. Courtesy of Bel Arte, London.

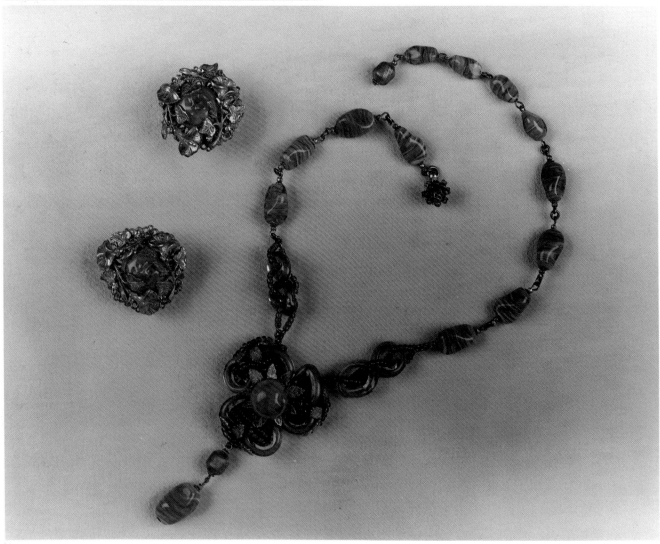

Two-strand translucent blue glass bead pendant necklace by Miriam Haskell. Courtesy of Bel Arte, London.

Stick pin with two floral clusters by Miriam Haskell; Green and clear stone-set fan-shaped pin marked Austria; Gold floral pin by Warner; Pendant floral and tortoise shell disc pin by Miriam Haskell. Courtesy of Cobra and Bellamy, London.

Translucent green glass bead necklace and pin by Miriam Haskell. Courtesy of Bel Arte, London.

Opposite:
Chain and pendant necklace and matching pair of earrings with pink glass stones, and a pair of blue glass and pearl earrings, all by Miriam Haskell. Courtesy of Bel Arte, London.

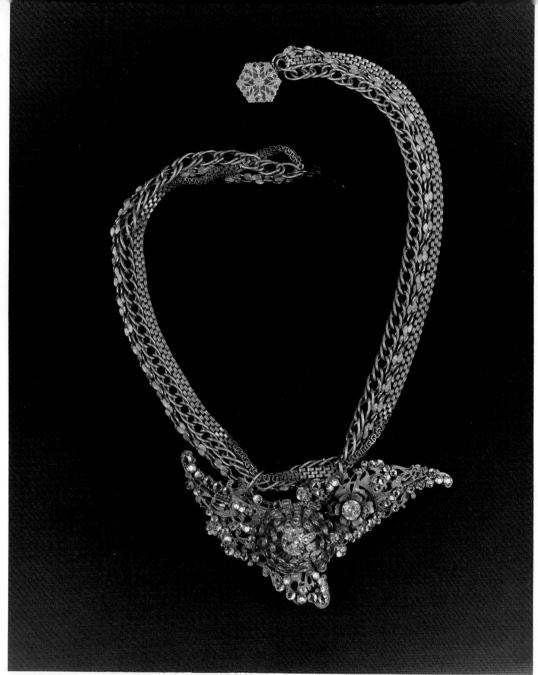

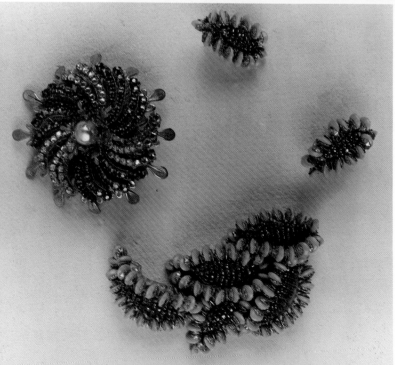

Triple chain necklace with cluster pendant by Miriam Haskell. Courtesy of Bel Arte, London.

Flowerhead pin with pearl center and leaf-shaped pinwith matching pair of earrings by Miriam Haskell. Courtesy of Bel Arte, London.

Triple chain necklace with floral pendant set
with pearls and bearing the horseshoe label of
Miriam Haskell. Courtesy of Bel Arte, London.

1950s

As though trying to establish a completely new style of their own, most designers of clothing at the beginning of the next decade, the 1950s, went through many revivals of old styles before settling down to a comfortable identity. As more relaxed lifestyles took hold, and music through the radio invited parties, cocktails were made popular and cocktail parties became the common form of entertainment. For these parties, dresses usually had lower-cut necklines which framed that most important piece of jewelry: the necklace. Matching sets were designed altogether but usually sold

Necklace of cast gilded metal in the forms of swans and shaped clear and white stones by Grosse for Christian Dior, circa 1953; shown with matching earrings and bracelet of seed pearls, pearls and glass beads, Corocraft by Coro, early 1950s.

separately to enable the customers to coordinate as they preferred.

The quality and volume of costume jewelry produced in this decade reached extremely high levels for not only were there more manufacturers, the public was becoming very particular. The fine quality of the leading designers was copied and challenged, and the field thus grew in both directions.

Flower basket pin by Christian Dior, red and clear pin which is unmarked, and flowerhead pin with green center by Ciner, 1950s.

Necklace of graduated clear rhinestones by Christian Dior, turquoise and clear pendant necklace is unmarked, graduated brown stone necklace is unmarked, 1950s.

Matching necklace, pin, and pair of earrings of brass and round and teardrop rhinestones by Christian Dior, circa 1953.

Dior

When Christian Dior opened his salon with the "New Look" in 1947, he provided a challenge to the older designers and an inspiration to the young. His success was both rapid and lasting, for the name became associated with only the highest standards of design and materials. Unfortunately, Dior only lived for ten years after his great initial success, but his company had begun to license its name to hand-picked design and manufacturing firms before he died in 1957, and they continue to license products today. The German firm of Grosse made jewelry for Dior from 1953, and Mitchel Maer of England made many Dior pieces in the early 1950s as well. The quality has not suffered through the years for the standards for the name have been kept very high.

Three necklaces and three bracelets of two, three and five strands of pearls in a line named PERLES "EAU DOUCE" by Christian Dior, early 1950s.

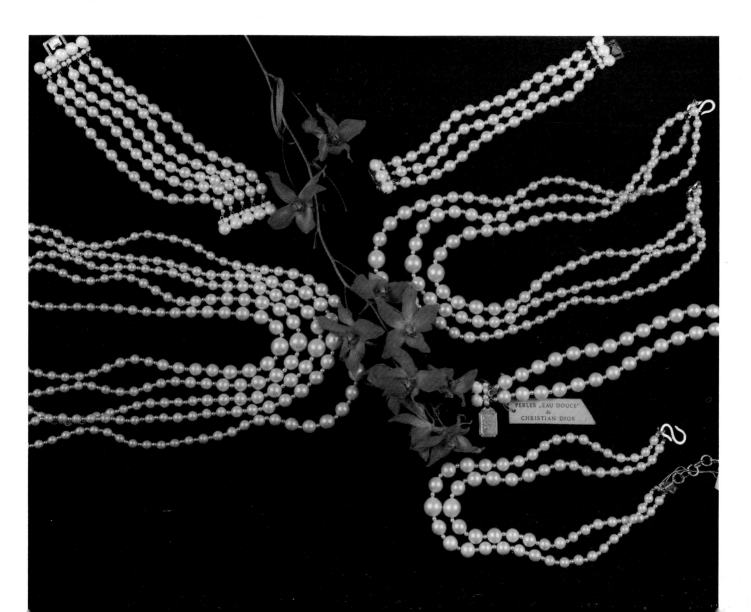

Matching triple-strand necklace and bracelet labeled "CALCUTTA de CHRISTIAN DIOR," 1959; and a bracelet of blue and purple stones which is unmarked.

Matching earrings and necklace of citrine glass and pearls, and a wisteria brooch of purple glass and graduated Baroque pearls, both by Christian Dior, early 1950s. Courtesy of Cobra and Bellamy, London.

Rhinestone star pin (1959), two pendant necklaces and a bracelet with colored glass beads and pearls (all 1960) by Christian Dior.

Matching necklace, bracelet, and pair of earrings of purple glass with round and tear-drop pearls by Christian Dior. Courtesy of Bel Arte, London.

Three-strand pearl necklace with floral cluster pendant and clasp set with rhinestones, and two pins of pave-set rhinestones and teardrop pearls pendant designed as a conch shell and a swordfish, by Mitchel Maer for Christian Dior, early 1950s.

Three triple-strand glass bead necklaces: brown beads marked "foreign," white beads labeled "BIARRITZ" de CHRISTIAN DIOR, green beads labeled "TOSCA de CHRISTIAN DIOR," all 1959.

Maer

American-born entrepreneur Mitchel Maer moved to London in the late 1930s to set up a manufacturing base for costume jewelry. He hired good designers and experimented with various machinery to produce metal castings. His firm, first called "Metalplastics" and later "Mitchel Maer," made a wide range of industrial castings as well as jewelry styles. In 1952, Christian Dior licensed Mitchel Maer to make the first jewelry for the Dior collection, and what stunning pieces they were. The designs were based on antique jewelry of Victorian, Georgian and earlier European creations. These pieces were marked "Christian Dior by Mitchel Maer." He also produced his own range of jewelry in a similar style. The jewelry manufacturing company went into bankruptcy in 1956. Mitchel Maer jewelry is highly desirable, extremely rare and very valuable today.

Necklace of twisted gold chain and delicate floral cluster by Mitchel Maer, early 1950s, and a bracelet of pearls and clustered panel by Mitchel Maer for Christian Dior.

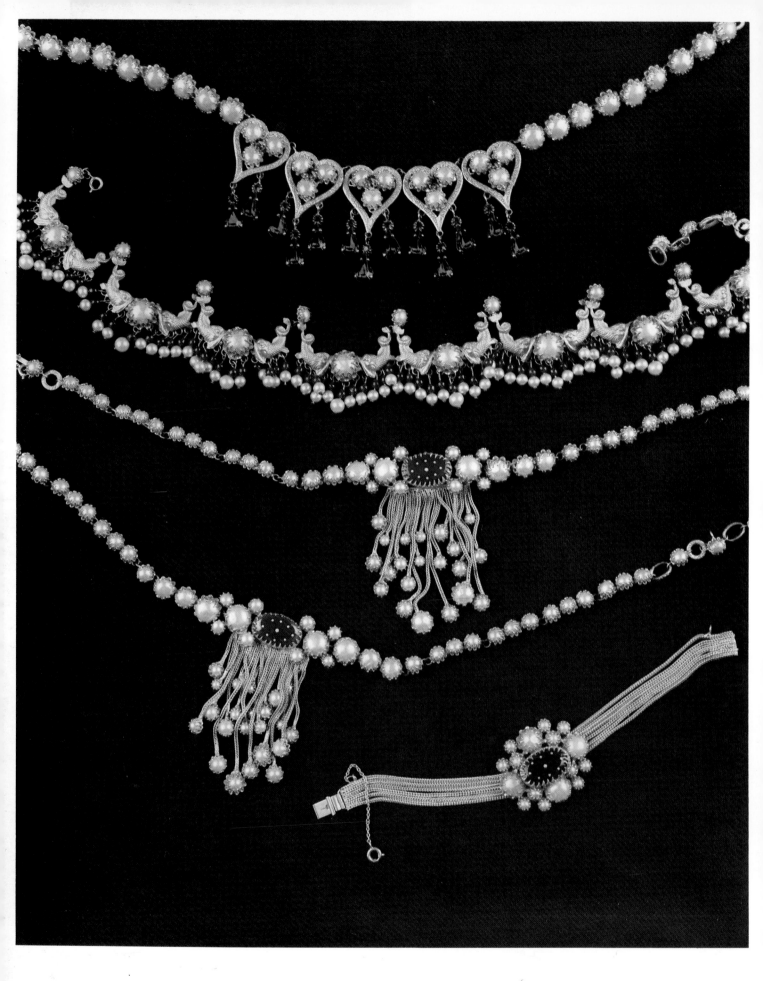

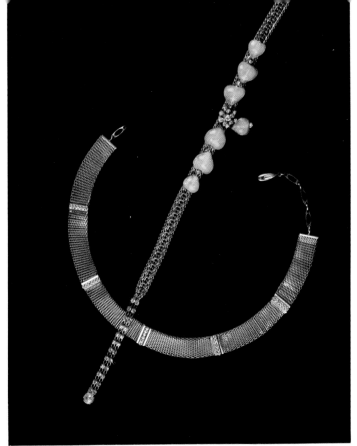

Opposite:
Four necklaces and bracelet with gold chain and pearls in imaginative designs by Mitchel Maer for Christian Dior.

Choker of gold chain and moonstones by Mitchel Maer, 1953; chain mail necklace by Henkel and Grosse, 1954.

Five bracelets and pin by Mitchel Maer for Christian Dior, early 1950s.

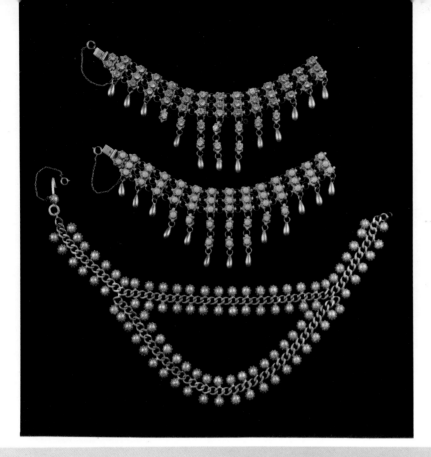

Necklace and two bracelets of gilded metal chain and prong-set stones by Mitchel Maer for Christian Dior, early 1950s.

Three necklaces of prong-set glass stones by Mitchel Maer for Christian Dior, early 1950s.

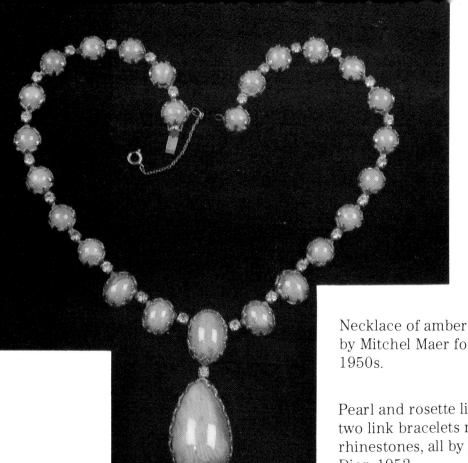

Necklace of amber-like glass and rhinestones by Mitchel Maer for Christian Dior, early 1950s.

Pearl and rosette linked fringe necklace, and two link bracelets mixing cabochons and rhinestones, all by Mitchel Maer for Christian Dior, 1953.

Matching set including necklace, pair of earrings, brooch, and bracelet made with colored glass stones throughout by Grosse for Christian Dior, 1955.

Opposite:
Necklace of blue cabochons, pearls and shaped clear stones, 1963; pair of earrings of white stones in the forms of butterflies, 1958; and delicate lace necklace of colored and clear stones, late 1950s, all by Grosse for Christian Dior.

Henkel & Grosse

In many ways the firm of Henkel & Grosse (now called Grosse Jewels) of Pforzheim, Germany may be regarded as one of the most important costume jewelers of all time. First organized in 1907 by Florentin Grosse (1878-1953) and Heinrich Henkel (1876 -1941), it produced gold settings for the jewelry trade. After the First World War, the company reorganized under Grosse's sons Artur and Adalbert Grosse who have led it since the 1930s to supply a complete global market. To have produced collections which catered to world tastes and fashions, moving all the time to the newest technology and marketing techniques, is a staggering achievement.

After Mitchel Maer, Henkel & Grosse was chosen to manufacture Christian Dior jewelry in 1955. From that time on, four collections each year had to be created. Their Christian Dior collections are noted today by the quality created for

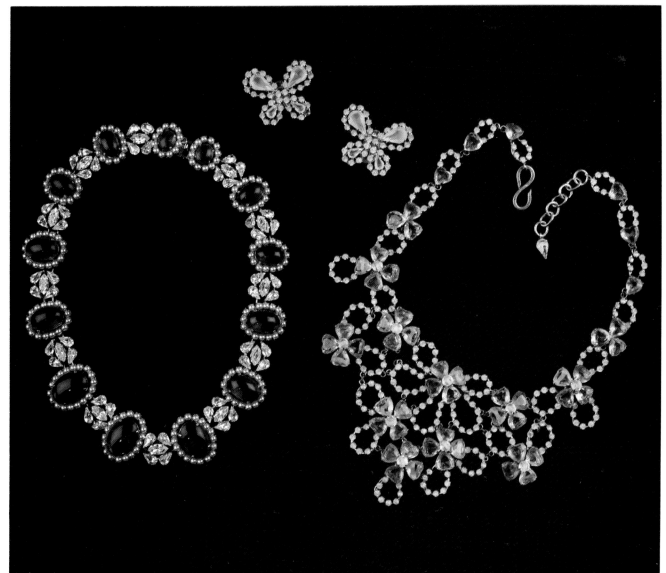

"haute couture." The unique use of beautiful color juxtapositions were avante-garde for the time.

Grosse jewelry from the 1940s and 1950s is characterized by bold, uniquely designed soldered pressings which are beautifully plated and polished. In the 1950s they were noted particularly for their work with "Milanese" chain and mesh, and their work in this field has never been equalled. Such pieces were made almost as well as their real gold counterparts. From the late 1960s to the present they are known for superb designs from cast molds as well.

Since 1958, Grosse has signed and dated each piece they made, whether from the Grosse or the Dior collections. The early pieces from both ranges are highly collectable and very valuable.

Although Adalbert Grosse has died, Artur Grosse is still as active as ever acting as president of the company, and the next generation is led in this business by Bert Grosse.

Basket of flowers pin by Eisenhart for Grosse, 1959; pear-drop pin of green stones, 1964; asymmetrical stone-studded pin, 1962; pearl drop and gold necklace, mid-1950s; purple graduated stone necklace, 1962, all Grosse for Christian Dior.

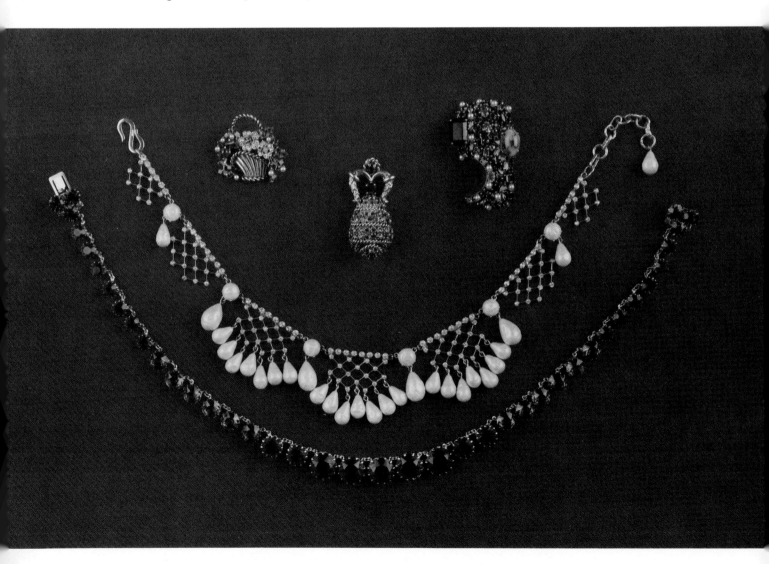

Matching set of pin, necklace and earrings of purple glass and pendant glass drops, 1960, and a triple-strand necklace of graduated orange stones and beads, 1959, both by Grosse for Christian Dior.

Necklace of colored stones with knotted front, 1962, and pendant necklace of silver chain and glass beads, both by Grosse for Christian Dior.

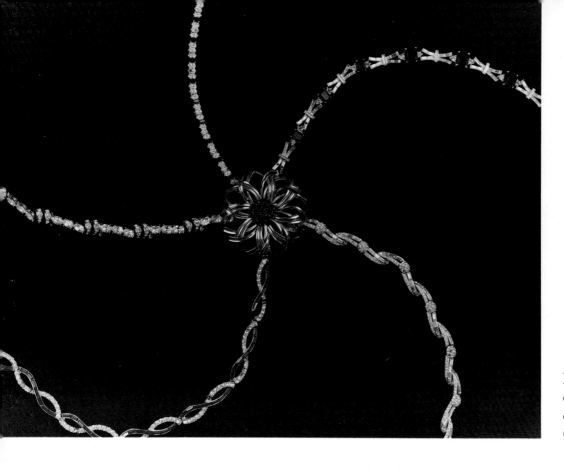

Five rhinestone-set chokers, 1960s, and a pin of intricate gold wire by Grosse, 1961.

Pair of earrings with red and green cabochons, 1971; small jeweled purse with cabochons, 1966, both by Grosse for Christian Dior; and a pair of dangle earrings with blue stones, unmarked.

Pair of earrings, 1965; pin with blue dangle, 1967; four-leaf pin, 1968; and flower pin, 1968, all by Grosse.

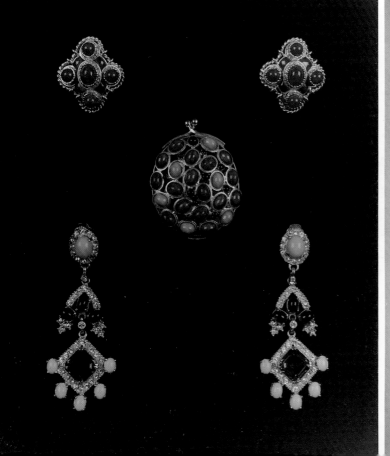

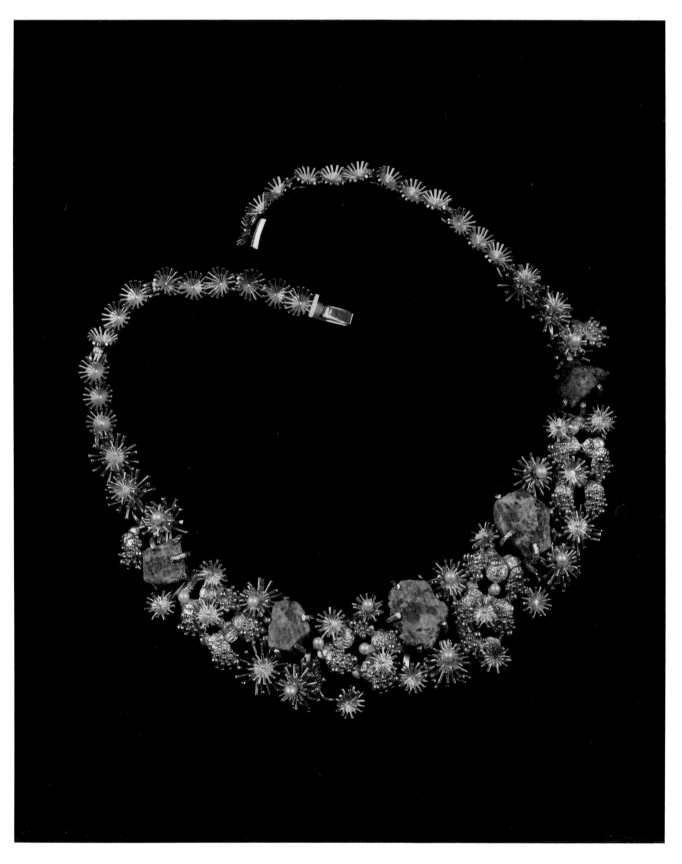

Necklace of gold work, five rock chunks and
small pearls by Grosse, mid-1960s.

Nine pairs of metal earrings by Henkel &
Grosse from the late 1950s.

Necklace and earrings of branch coral design with green stones, 1957; necklace of gold chain with large glass plates in frames, 1972; choker with small turquoise stones, 1958, all by Grosse.

Gold feather pin with small blue stones, 1962; pin with blue rock chunk, 1966; pin with marcasite chunk and gold and turquoise stones, unmarked; pear-shaped pearls and gold pin, 1967; gold dragon bracelet, 1968; round pin with colored pearls and gold, 1968; gold knot pin with rhinestones for Christian Dior, 1968; all by Grosse.

Delicate necklace of gold work and pearl links in floral design, and a pin of pink rock and gold nuggets, both by Grosse for Christian Dior, 1966.

Five figural pins of gold plated metal, the enameled rose bud with marcasites by Hermann Schwager, circa 1955; four by Grosse: bird with red eye, 1965; bull, 1968; green plant, 1965; gold bird, 1959.

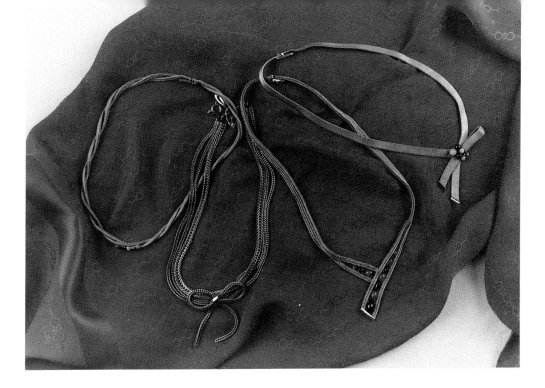

Four gold chain necklaces made in 1962 by Grosse, the one with the bowknot made for Christian Dior.

Pierced disc pendant necklace with gold chain and a pair of earrings, and a small pendant necklace with chain tassel, 1973, for Christian Dior, all by Grosse.

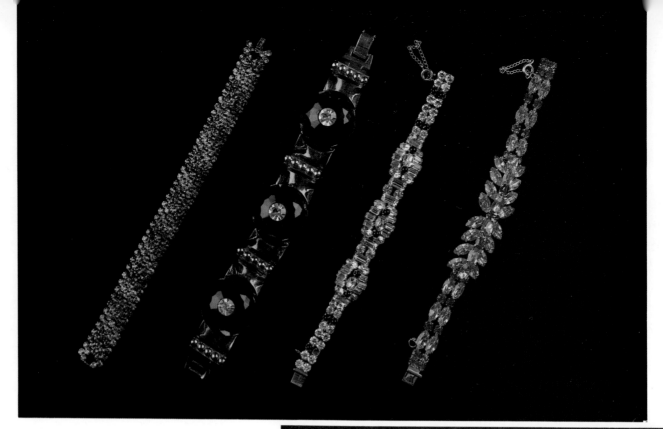

Four bracelets of very different characters, but all made with rhinestones: brown and yellow diagonally set stones, 1960s; large brown stones encasing clear stones, and mounted in brass, 1940s; clear bagettes and brilliants accented with black cabochons, 1950s; blue marquise and pink brilliants in a cluster design, 1950s.

Kramer

Founded in New York in 1943 by Louis Kramer as "Kramer Jewelry Creations," this firm sold costume jewelry until the late 1970s. Kramer was a famous name in the 1940s and 1950s. Different manufacturers created exclusive designs for this company whose range started at the lower level and rose to fine pieces in their "Real Look" collections. At the lower end, the jewelry was similar in concept to Coro's jewelry, but a good inexpensive range was made in all "gold" pressings. It was a wide range, reflecting especially the times and fashions of the U.S.A. in the post-war years. All pieces are interesting for this reason, but their "Real Look" pieces, which were usually signed, are way above the rest in quality due to their hand-set finish in rhodium plate.

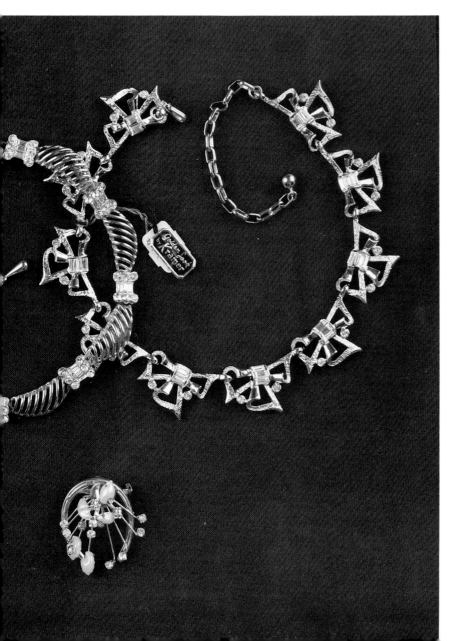

"Diamond Look" choker of rhinestone rings, 1955; gold choker with rhinestones, early 1950s; "Golden Look" bowknot necklace, 1955; round pearl and rhinestone pin, 1955; and horseshoe pin with baroque pearls and rhinestones, 1955, all by Kramer of New York.

"Golden Look" pin and pair of earrings with pearls and rhinestones on gold wires; pin of looped golden wires and pearl tips, 1954; pin with three flowerheads of rhinestones, 1953; all by Kramer of New York; and gold bow pin by Henkel & Grosse, early 1950s.

Matching necklace and earrings of pearls, rhinestones and gold; and link bracelet of pearls, rhinestones and gold, both by Kramer of New York; and star-shaped pin of rhinestones, gold and pearls marked P. Monelle.

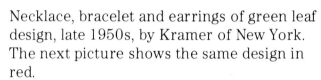

Necklace, bracelet and earrings of green leaf design, late 1950s, by Kramer of New York. The next picture shows the same design in red.

"Golden Look" necklace, 1955; pair of petal cluster gold-plated earrings; "Golden Look" bracelet, 1954; circle pin of twisted rope design, mid-1950s, all by Kramer of New York.

Link bracelet of gold and brown stones in a rope design; bracelet of six oval pearl-studded links; matching set of earrings, bracelet and choker of gold leaves and rhinestones, all by Kramer of New York.

Matching set of pearl and gold rope jewelry including a choker, bracelet and earrings; and another set of jewelry, this design with green leaves and gold including a choker, bracelet, pin and earrings, both sets by Kramer of New York.

1960s

Costume jewelry in the 1960s became liberated from traditional designs. Many craft-artists made self-styled pieces from any material they could find including papier-mâché, enamels, plastics and glass. Influenced by the space exploration programs of Russia and the United States, designers explored new ideas. The dream of world peace pervaded the youth who made pendant necklaces of badges and crosses popular in bright and contrasting colors. Modern music evolved into rock bands of many types, with Elvis Presley and later the Beatles becoming leaders in popularity. When they wore jewelry, that style became sought-after overnight.

German choker of red, green and blue glass beads, circa 1969; and an enameled cross pendant necklace, circa 1969-70, by Jomaz.

Traditional-style designers fared less well during this decade when tastes began to change away from delicate and well made jewelry to the bright and bold designs regardless of quality. In fact, consumers were more typically interested in quantity than quality, and so the lower-priced lines sold much better than the high-priced lines. This trend spelled doom for some of the old-time manufacturers.

Pair of earrings by Coro with silver backing and baguette rhinestones around pearl; three-strand pearl bracelet with rhinestone cluster, unmarked; three pair of earrings with gold and rhinestone clusters around pearl, unmarked, all early 1960s.

Two gold and rhinestone-studded pins of bold designs, early 1960s.

Lace collar necklace with gold and brown stones, unmarked, early 1960s.

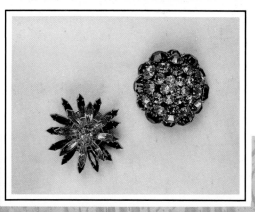

Two gold and brown stone pins, unmarked, early 1960s. Courtesy of N. Bloom & Son, London.

Brown bead lace collar, unmarked, early 1960s.

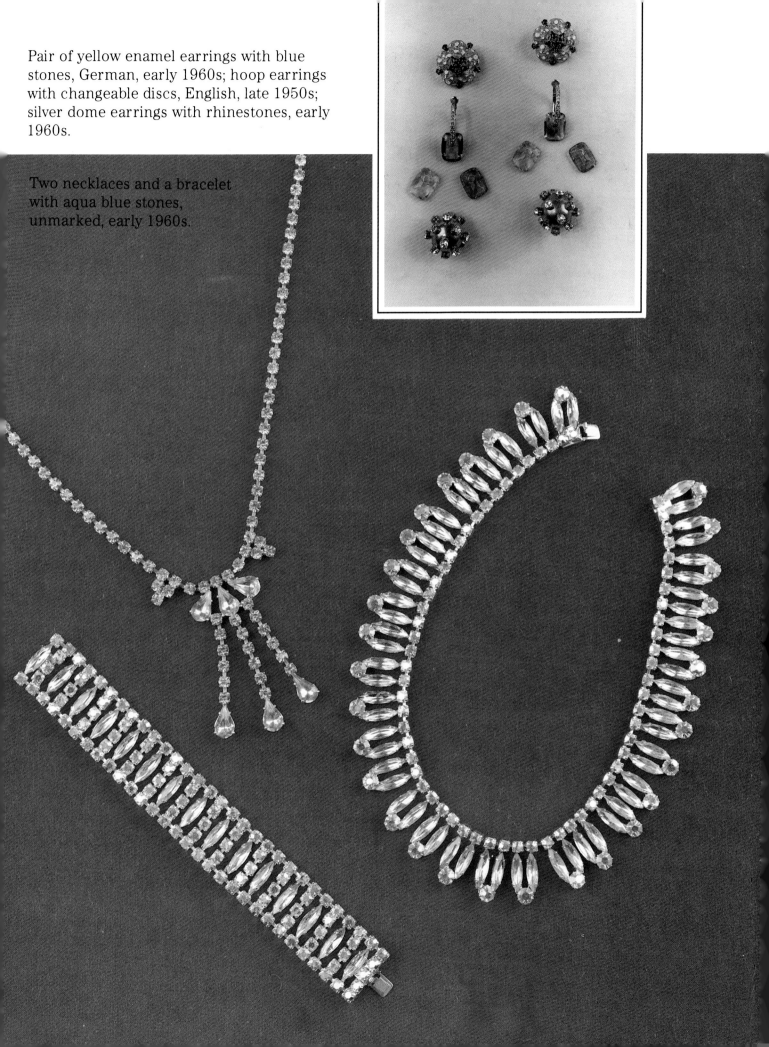

Pair of yellow enamel earrings with blue stones, German, early 1960s; hoop earrings with changeable discs, English, late 1950s; silver dome earrings with rhinestones, early 1960s.

Two necklaces and a bracelet with aqua blue stones, unmarked, early 1960s.

Givenchy

French designer Hubert de Givenchy opened his own design house in 1952, built upon the traditional European styles. His jewelry was inspired by the sleek lines of the Art Deco style which was still popular in some circles into the 1960s.

Opposite:
Two pendant necklaces with lapis-lazuli type stones by Jomaz; and a choker of gold chain, blue enamel and rhinestones, 1960s.

Pendant necklace of glass beads and pendant with rhinestones by Givenchy, early 1960s; and three link bracelets, each marked France, 1940s.

Black, red and green pendants for chain necklaces, all by Givenchy, early 1960s; and a red apple with serpent pendant by Panetta.

Three pendant necklaces of gold-plated metal, enamels, colored and clear stones, the two resembling flowers by D'Orlan and the round medallion being unmarked.

Gold pin with three green stones by D'Orlan, circa 1970; leaf-shaped pin with rhinestones, circa 1961; floral group pin of gold and white stones by Castlecliff, mid-1960s; gold and topaz pin, circa 1970.

Jomaz

Joseph Mazer and his brother began manufacturing costume jewelry in 1927 in New York under the label "Mazer Brothers." From the mid-1950s they used the names "Joseph Mazer" and "Jomaz." Their jewelry was made in large volumes and many varieties for the mid-priced market until the mid-1970s, when the firm closed.

Five gold-plated pins set with rhinestones by Jomaz, 1960s.

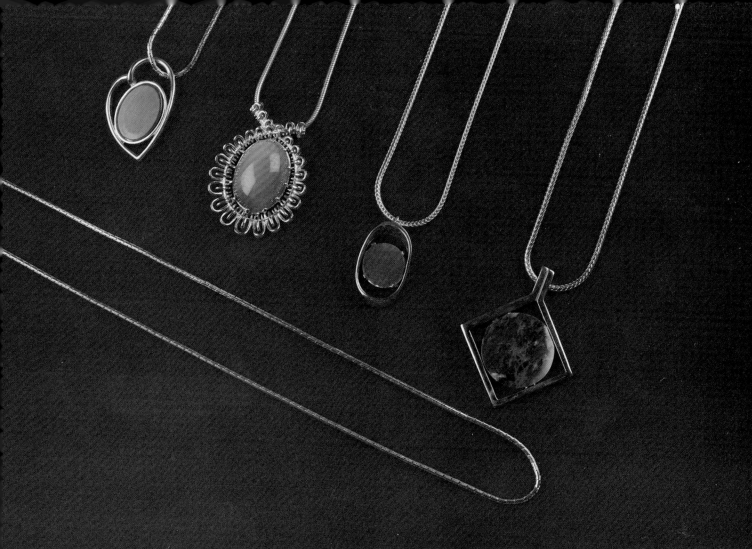

Pendant necklaces with various chains: heart-shaped with green stone, Jomaz; large oval green stone in pendant; small oval green stone in pendant by Joseph Mazer; blue round stone in pendant by Jomaz; all mid-1960s.

Enameled cross pin/pendant, and pendant with matching earrings of enameled medallions by Jomaz, mid-1960s.

Opposite:
Six pendant necklaces: leaf shape by Jomaz; yellow medallion by Joseph Mazer; green enameled cross by Jomaz; gold cross with silver decoration by Jomaz; Faberge-style egg pendant unmarked; red heart pendant unmarked; all mid-1960s.

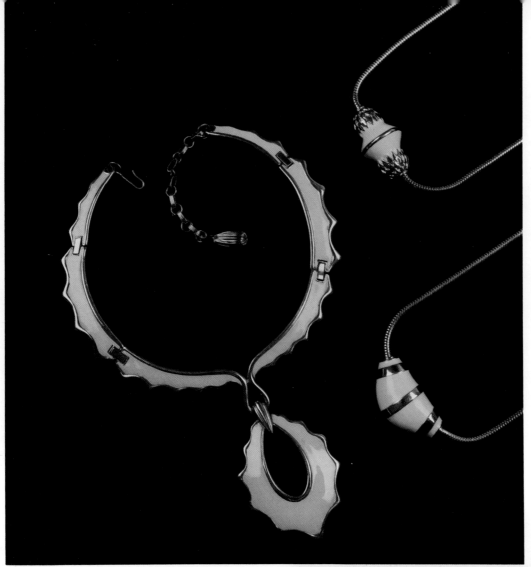

Two pendant necklaces and a choker with pendant all made with enamel and gold plating by Jomaz, mid-1960s.

Pin as a rope knot with pave ends, pair of dangle earrings set with colored cabochons, and enameled bangle bracelet with rhinestones, all by Jomaz, 1960s.

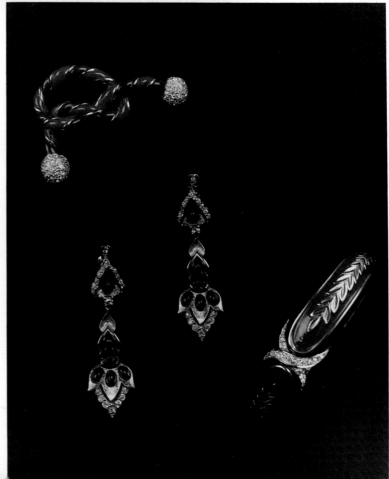

Group of jewelry by Jomaz from the 1960s: bracelet with white enamel, green carved jadelike stone pendant, earrings with three green stones, large pin with blue enamel and green stones, pair of earrings with two large green stones, and flowerhead pin with coral and green stones.

Group of jewelry by Jomaz including five pins, a bracelet and one pair of earrings, a stunning array of artistic designs well made.

Enameled cuff bracelet by Jomaz; and necklace with matching bracelet of red enamel and pave rhinestones by Joseph Mazer, 1970. The blue necklace in the photograph below is a variation of the red set here.

Necklace of linked ovals with blue enamel and pave rhinestones, 1970; bracelet of linked blue cabochons and rhinestone links, and one pair of earrings of blue stones and gold plated metal accents, all by Joseph Mazer.

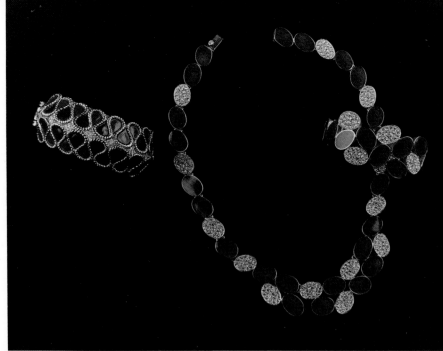

Matching necklace, bracelet, and pair of earrings of enamel and rhinestone leaf-shaped links by Jomaz.

Two necklaces of chain links and enamel decoration of very different characters, both by Jomaz.

Four pins of far-differing designs yet all made in the mid-1960s: swirl design of clear rhinestones, circa 1963; bold pin of gold with large red stone and clear rhinestones by Jomaz; and two pins with rhinestones and red or blue stones, 1965.

Flowerhead pin and matching earrings with rhinestones and blue cabochon centers; circular leafy branch pin of rhinestones surrounding an amethyst colored stone; and a pin in the form of a bouquet of blue stones and rhinestones, all by Jomaz.

Matching set of jewelry including pearl, enamel and rhinestone necklace, hinged bracelet and earrings, made by Jomaz in 1973 in a variety of colors: coral, aqua, dark green, and grey with grey pearls.

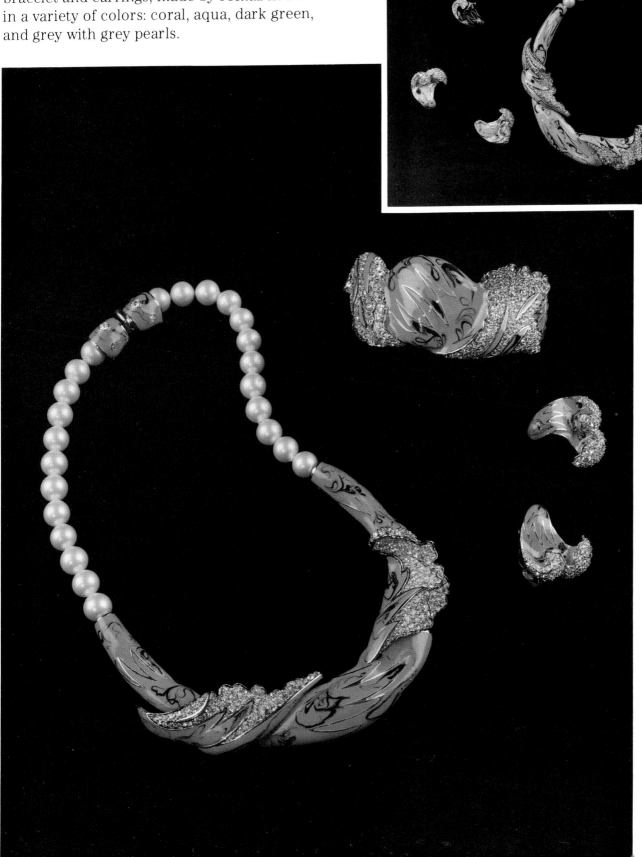

Figurals

Jewelry representing birds, animals, and people engaged in sports and other recreational activities are popularly referred to as "figurals," and they were made profusely in the 1960s and 1970s by Jomaz and other firms. Often whimsical, always decorative, they added a light touch to casual jewelry.

Penguin pin, unmarked; owl pendant by Trifari; silver owl pin by Grosse, 1971; green macaw pin, unmarked; owl with large eyes pin by Jomaz, 1970, and gold bird head pin, unmarked.

A group of figural pins from the 1960s: jumping deer by Coro, black dachshund by D'Orlan, white enameled lobster by Trifari, double horseheads clip with unclear mark, silver elephant is unmarked, black whale, deer drinking water by Coro, single horse head is unmarked, and ram with corkscrew horns by Castlecliff.

Group of jewelry from the late 1960s by Jomaz: pin designed as the back of a horse-drawn coach; black pearl necklace with crystal briolette pendants; coral-bellied owl, 1967; dark green enameled pin with rhinestones and cabochon amethyst-colored center, 1967; and white enameled lily of the valley pin.

Above:
Five figural pins: wirework firefly, and Punch by Grosse; Joker stick puppet by Jomaz, 1969; clown with umbrella has indistinct mark; and Scotty dog by Boucher.

Below:
The Buddah medallion pendant by Joseph Mazer is surrounded by four unmarked figural pins: kneeling blackamoor, turbaned head, woman's head with chain hair, and head armor with marcasite plumes.

Opposite:
Group of figural pins from the 1960s: bird head circle with pearl by Castlecliff, two black birds are unmarked, green and rhinestone bird is unmarked, palm tree by Castlecliff, gold donkey by Polcini, white donkey by Boucher, horsehead is unmarked, dog with chain tassel by Castlecliff, and sleeping cat by D'Orlan.

Seven whimsical figural pins by Jomaz, including a green-clad character and a dwarf from "Snow White."

Five pins representing flowers: violet bouquet by Jomaz; blue and clear flower by Christian Dior, 1960; green and clear stone flowerhead by Kramer of New York; red cabochon flower with pearl center by Boucher; and red invisibly-set tulip by Trifari, 1961.

Matching pin and pair of earrings with delicately-shaded green and yellow translucent stones by Jomaz.

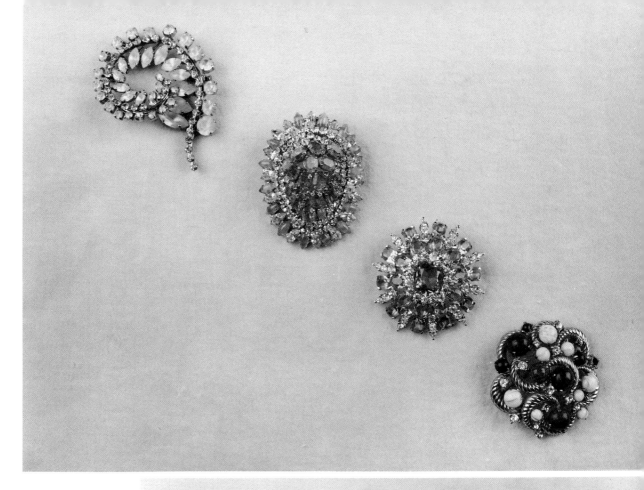

Clear and white stone scroll pin by Christian Dior, circa 1953; pink and clear stone shield-shaped pin by Christian Dior, 1968; green and yellow stone pin by Jomaz, 1970; and gold pin with blue and pink prong-set stones by Grosse, 1969.

Pin with small black flowers by Jomaz, circa 1968; round pin with dark blue stone center surrounded by red and white spiral setting by Boucher; and rhinestone pin with dark blue stone center by Polcini, 1964.

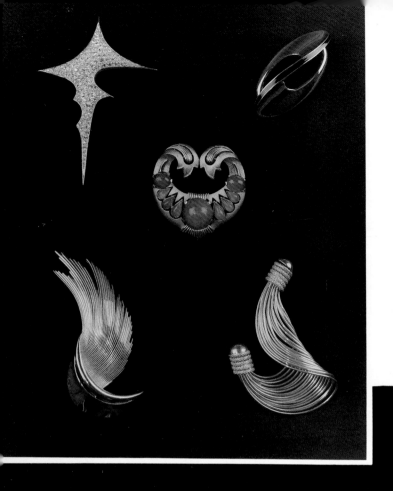

Opposite:
Flowers of many species were represented as pins in the 1960s by different makers: small gold and rhinestone pin, and the horse chestnut pin are unmarked, brown enameled set of pin and earrings are not marked, white enameled leaf by Jomaz, gold-plated tulip by Trifari, and gold-plated flowerhead with turquoise center is unmarked.

Five pins with freedom-seeking designs by different makers: rhinestone pave design by Jomaz, gold interlocked ovals with black enamel edge by Ciner, scrolling crescent with green stones, and all-gold feather-edge design both by Trifari, and gold wire pin which is unmarked.

Five figural pins by different makers: white enamel arrow, and large enameled Aztec-style bird both by Jomaz; witch's hat and broom, and wishbone with pearl both by Trifari; and mushroom by Castlecliff.

Six gold-washed and stone-set pins by Jomaz from the 1960s and 1970s.

Amorphous heart pin with white enamel and rhinestones, and a matching set of pin and pair of earrings with white stones, both by Jomaz.

Opposite:
Four pins and two pairs of earrings from the early 1970s by Jomaz.

Four pins from the late 1960s by Jomaz.

Free-form arrow of green and clear stones by Trifari, 1965; oval sunburst pin with turquoise center by Jomaz, 1970; feather edge pin by Jomaz, 1965; and white enamel and green stone tree trunk pin by Jomaz, 1970.

Polcini

In 1911, Ralph Polcini, a goldsmith from Italy, founded a costume jewelry manufacturing firm in New York which he named "Leading Jewelry". The business continued until 1949 when the firm was renamed "LEDO". When Ralph Polcini died in 1954, the company was inherited by his son Damon who, in 1960, renamed it "Polcini" and ran it until the late 1970s. After Damon Polcini died in 1984, his wife and three daughters kept the name alive, and since 1987 have produced new designs to join the old ones in a continuity of fine quality jewelry. The Polcini companies produced very good quality hand-set jewelry. Their designs were traditional and conservative with emphasis on restraint. A range of pieces with reconstituted opal was highly successful.

Opposite:
Five pins of plated-gold metal with rhinestones and "opals" in floral designs by Polcini.

Five pins of quite varied floral and bowknot designs by Polcini.

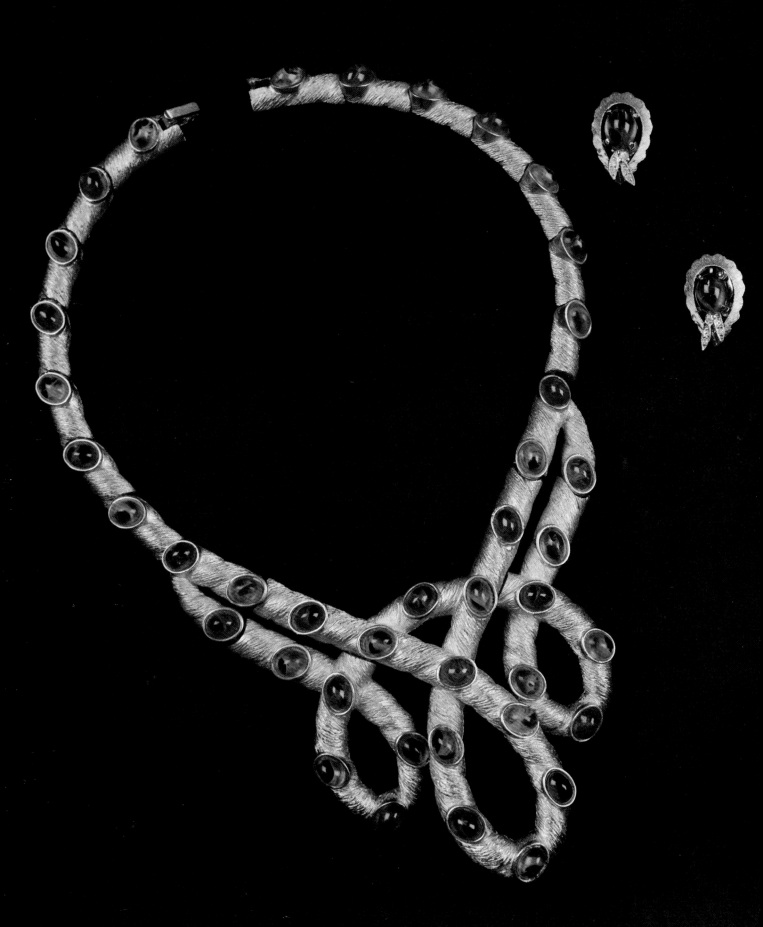

Trifari

Begun in New York in 1921 as "Trifari, Krussman & Fishel" by founders Gustavo Trifari, Leo F. Krussman, and Carl Fishel, this company first used the mark "T.K.F." to identify their jewelry.

French jewelry designer Alfred Philippe was hired to direct the design department, and from around 1925 all pieces were marked "Trifari." Philippe's designs were noted for their exquisite styling right up to the 1960s.

At all their price levels Trifari jewelry was beautifully made, their lacquering process to protect the plating being outstanding. Ninety percent of each collection was invariably styled on traditional yet fashionable motifs, and this part of their collections sold to the mass market in big stores all across the U.S.A. But it was the other ten percent that elevated Trifari to its preeminent place in the costume jewelry field.

The special jewelry by Trifari will be self-evident but all pieces are worth collecting. Inevitably the finest pieces are both rare and valuable.

Opposite:
Earrings of green glass stones in gold plated frame by Polcini, 1962; and necklace by Trifari.

Large and elegant flower pin of individual stones assembled by Trifari with practically none of the setting visible, circa 1960.
Courtesy of Cobra and Bellamy, London.

Opposite:
Group of jewelry made by Trifari: pair of colorful carnation earrings and matching pin with invisibly set stones; link bracelet of large green and clear stones; finger ring with black carved ram's head mount, 1960s; pin in the form of a cicada with rhinestone-studded body; exoticly designed swan pin with red enamel, carved jade-like panel and rhinestones. Courtesy of Cobra and Bellamy, London.

Pin replicating invisibly set sapphires in a leaf frond design with rhinestones by Trifari, circa 1961.

Matching set of earrings and pin of red invisibly set stones designed as a leaf frond, and a large pin of antique design with red stones around a shield of clear rhinestones, all by Trifari. Courtesy of Cobra and Bellamy, London.

Delightful group of seven pins: fluttering butterfly, unmarked; pave-set clear rhinestone exotic bird, unmarked; large bird with turquoise head and green body by Hattie Carnegie; blue enameled bee, pair of peacocks, and "clear-belly" sailfish, all by Trifari. Courtesy of Bel Arte, London.

Pastel enamel and green stone-set pin in floral design, unmarked; gold wirework floral pin with blue and clear stones, unmarked; bouquet pin of pastel stones and enameled leaves by Trifari.

Trifari pins of truly exquisite design and execution; tree of pave rhinestones with pink and blue stone leaves, and a cascade of pink flowers emerging from a gold flower pot. Courtesy of Cobra and Bellamy, London.

107

Flower head pin of great power by Alfred Phillipe for Trifari. Courtesy of Cobra and Bellamy, London.

Lyre bird pin by Trifari. Courtesy of Cobra and Bellamy, London.

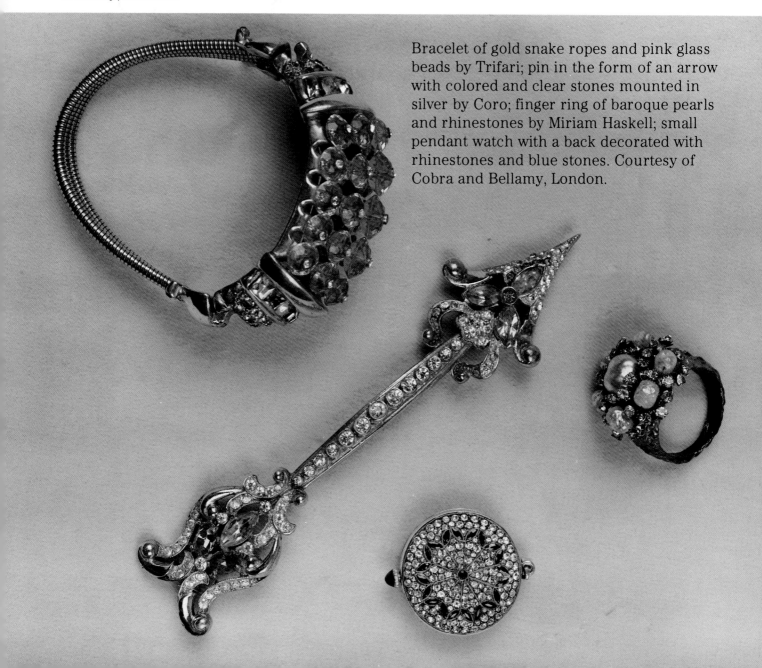

Bracelet of gold snake ropes and pink glass beads by Trifari; pin in the form of an arrow with colored and clear stones mounted in silver by Coro; finger ring of baroque pearls and rhinestones by Miriam Haskell; small pendant watch with a back decorated with rhinestones and blue stones. Courtesy of Cobra and Bellamy, London.

Four figural pins by Trifari, each beautifully detailed with rhinestones. Courtesy of Bel Arte, London.

Pair of earrings and matching double clip with glass beads and rhinestones by Trifari. Courtesy of Cobra and Bellamy, London.

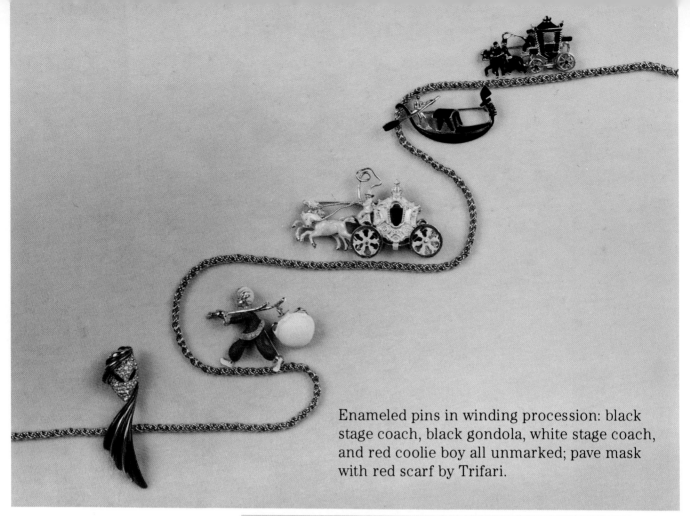

Enameled pins in winding procession: black stage coach, black gondola, white stage coach, and red coolie boy all unmarked; pave mask with red scarf by Trifari.

Pink stones assembled into a floral pin, unmarked; double blossom pin of gold with black centers by Boucher; iridescent marquise stones and drop pearls forming a leafy bough marked "Germany," circa 1955; apple pin pave set with green stones and rhinestones by Trifari.

Serpent pin in blue graduated stones and rhinestones with two red ribbed glass drops, and a double clip of blue and clear baguettes and rhinestones both by Trifari. Courtesy of Cobra and Bellamy, London.

Two pins and a bracelet of magnificent designs, the highest quality materials and superb workmanship by Trifari. Courtesy of Bel Arte, London.

All-rhinestone necklace of triple loops
enclosing drops by Kramer of New York; and a
five-strand necklace of green glass beads,
pearls and rhinestones by Trifari.

Opposite:
Earrings and matching pendant necklace of
blue stones mounted in a globular setting,
1964-1965; gold and rhinestone link bracelet
of five rows, 1963; gold and green enamel link
bracelet, 1963-1964; feather-like gold and
rhinestonelink bracelet, 1967, all by Trifari.

Large pin of pave rhinestones and pearls
forming two lilys; bracelet of purple stones
and rhinestones in a cluster design; bracelet
of rhinestones, pearls and enamel in a cluster
design, all by Trifari. Courtesy of N. Bloom &
Son, London.

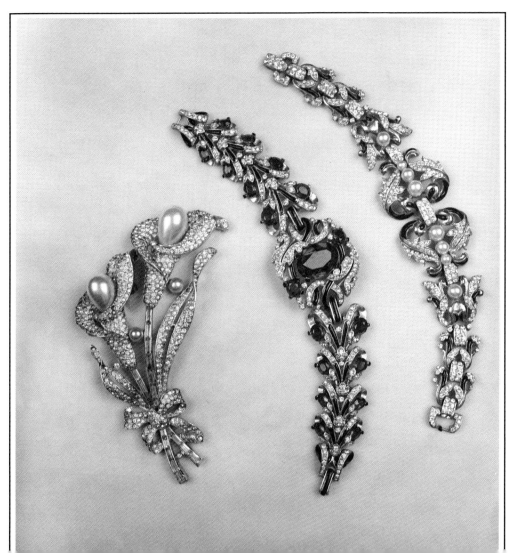

113

Triple pendant necklace of brushed gold finish and chains of fringe by Trifari, circa 1965; and pendant necklace of gold squares and lapis-lazuli stones by Grosse for Christian Dior, 1971.

Two bracelets of brown plastic links and green plastic links, and a pendant necklace of brown beads and gold chain, all by Trifari.

Opposite:
Seven pendant necklaces by Trifari from the late 1960s when this form of jewelry was so popular.

Three completely differently-shaped pins all designed by Trifari. Courtesy of Bel Arte, London.

Necklace and matching pair of earrings of Florentine gold ribbon loops and blue stones, and a bracelet of sculpted gold and white stones designed to appear soft although it is made in metal, all by Trifari.

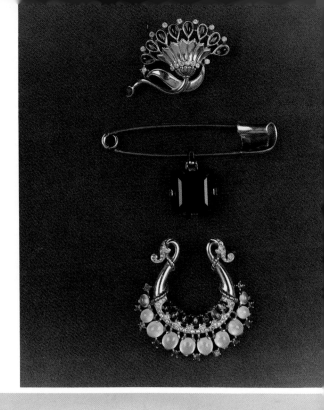

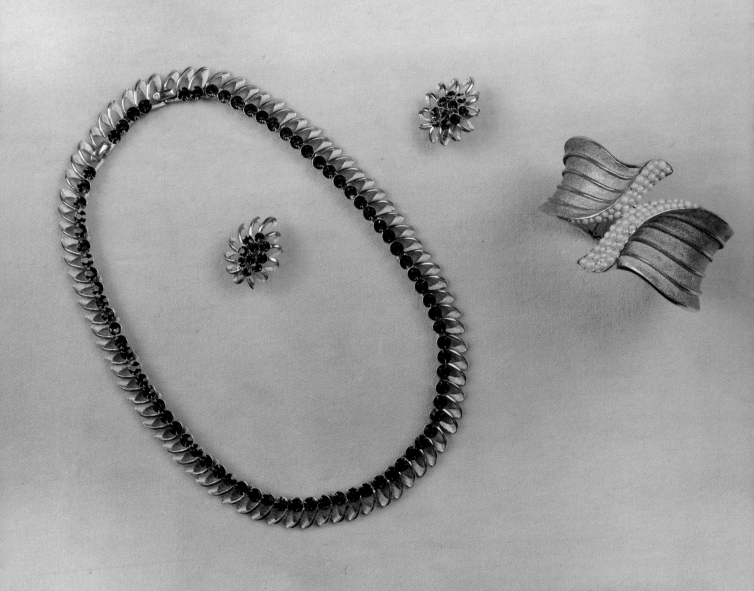

"Floraleaf" pin and matching earrings of gold-plated metal and light blue carved stones designed as leaves, 1948; large pin of blue carved stones, plated metal and rhinestones; pair of earrings of green cabochon stones and plated metal, all by Trifari. Courtesy of Cobra and Bellamy, London.

Gold-plated pin resembling a conch shell, unmarked; necklace with gold chain and green and clear stones; matching set of necklace and earrings with heart-shaped metal links and rhinestones, both necklaces by Trifari. Courtesy of Bel Arte, London.

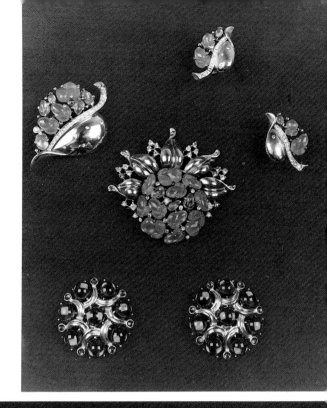

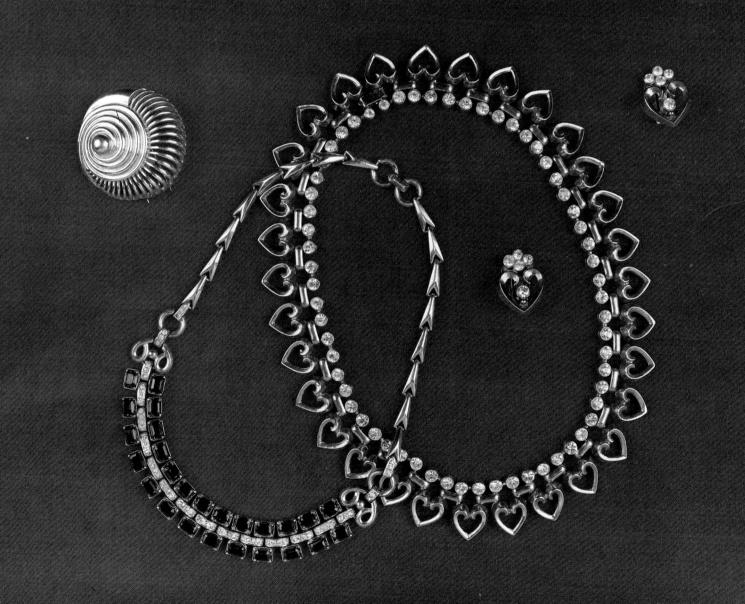

Opposite:
Two necklaces of white enameled metal and metal links by Trifari.

Group of jewelry by Trifari: feather-like pin, 1963-1964; openwork mushroom pin with rhinestones, 1965; pin of three ginko leaves and pearls, circa 1960; two mushrooms and turquoise stones mounted as a pin; pair of earrings designed as pea pods, 1965; and gold-plated metal leaves pin, late 1960s.

White enamel star-shaped pin by Trifari; two unmarked chain necklaces with white links or beads; pair of earrings by Ciner designed as enameled buckles; white enamel pin of intersecting ribbon design by Trifari.

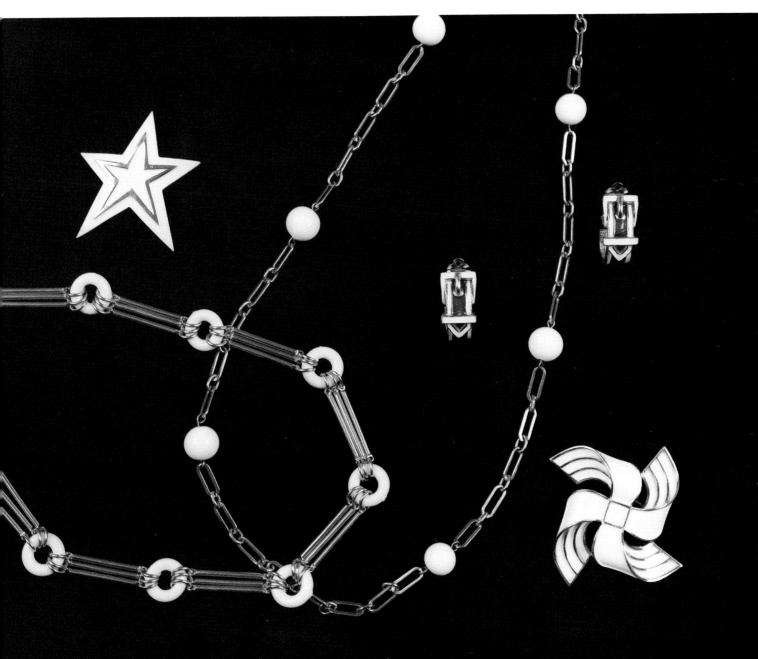

Opposite:
Matching pin and pair of earrings of large green cabochons and clear marquise and baguette stones by Trifari. Courtesy of Cobra and Bellamy, London.

Seven finger rings of Art Deco and modern designs: square black stone with rhinestones, 1970; two black triangles by Trifari, 1965; others unmarked.

Keys to unlock a heart is the theme of this jewelry including a pendant necklace by Trifari, and two plated metal and rhinestone pins which are unmarked.

Pin and matching earrings of leaf shape set with turquoise stones by Trifari; flowerhead pin of wirework and rhinestones by Castlecliff; link bracelet of white enamel, turquoise and blue cabochons by Trifari; and leaf-shaped pin by Sandor with openwork and turquoise stones.

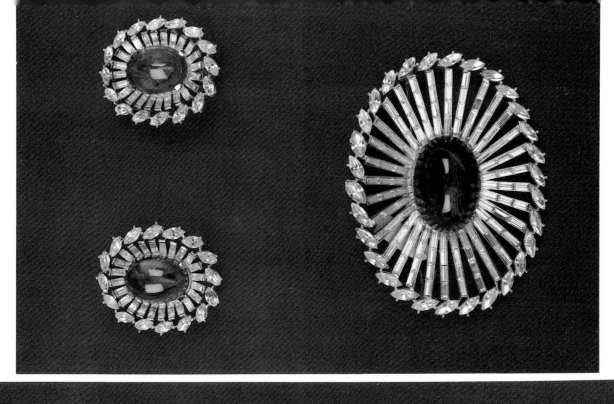

Bracelet of pave-set turquoise, red and blue stones by Trifari. Courtesy of Cobra and Bellamy, London.

Group of jewelry made by Trifari; oval clip with carved blue and pink stones; turquoise and clear stones assembled as a leaf frond; link choker of rope design with rhinestones; pin of intersecting circles and ribbon; and a pin of pearls and rhinestones resembling a white tornado. Courtesy of Bel Arte, London.

1970s

Popular fashions in the 1970s returned to soft designs of long skirts, small-print fabrics, and earth tones. Peasant dresses and sandals became the customary dress for liberal-thinking youth who wanted liberation from all hard-edge forms of social pressures. Sports and fitness became fashionable. The jewelry which many people accompanied with these styles was more conservative than the bold styles of the 1960s, more quaint, old fashioned and unostentatious. The average woman wore less jewelry and wore it less often. This trend was not good for the costume jewelry business at large. Many of the established companies that had grown large in the 1950s and 1960s found they could not sell sufficient jewelry to support large staffs and elaborate machinery. Also, several of the

Four rather quaint figural pins of plant life themes from the 1970s, unmarked.

Mineral specimens mounted as jewelry in four rings and three pendants, unmarked, probably from Germany.

leaders in the field were reaching retirement age. When cost-cutting included reducing the price of materials for the jewelry, lesser stones, more enamels and simpler designs were tried. As manufactured jewelry became less costly, craft-artists used very inexpensive materials to form decorations of new and experimental types, and they became popular. Many of the costume manufacturing firms closed or significantly diminished production in these years.

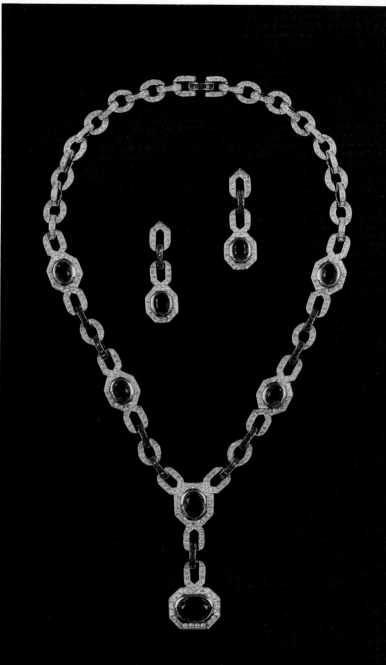

Pendant necklace with metal chain cord and jeweled pendant, late 1970s.

Necklace and matching pair of earrings designed as a municipal badge of office chain with pendant.

Opposite:
Necklace of gold and coral rods and beads, circa 1970.

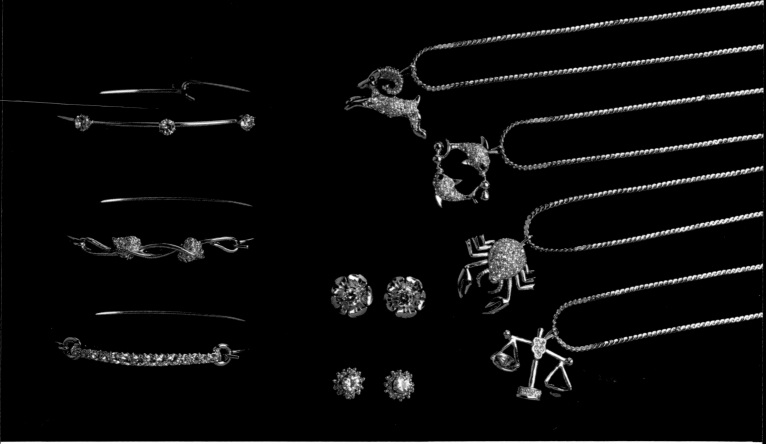

Three rhinestone-set bracelets of gold-plated wire, two pair of button-style earrings, and four rhinestone-set pendants representing signs of the Zodiac, all from 1979. Photograph courtesy of Fior, London.

Choker of gold and rhinestone-set links with green oval cabochons, late 1970s.

Opposite:
Gold plated wristwatch, floral cluster pendant and matching pin of pearls and rhinestones, all from 1979. Photograph courtesy of Fior, London.

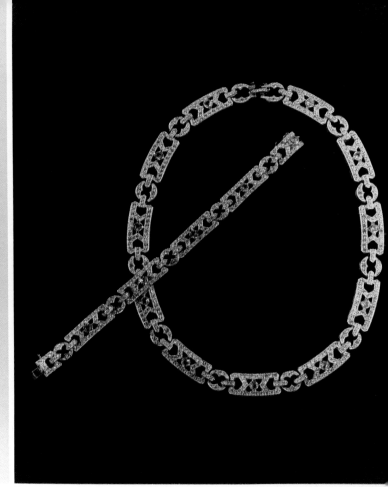

Pendant necklace of amethyst and clear stones set into links and supporting a large amethyst-colored drop, late 1970s or early 1980s.

Necklace and matching bracelet of rhinestone-set links, late 1970s.

Hinged necklace and matching earrings of aqua stones and rhinestones set into plated gold metal, late 1970s.

Opposite:
Group of turquoise and rhinestone jewelry including two sets of necklace, bracelet and earrings; two sets of neck chains and earrings; and two pairs of earrings; 1980. Photograph courtesy of Fior.

Ciner

In 1931 the Ciner jewelry firm, begun in 1892 by Emanuel Ciner in New York, began to make costume jewelry in response to its growing popularity at that time. Ciner designers had very high standards for hand-set jewelry which was sold in carefully screened shops. The business has continued to the present and the range of pieces is immense. A particular style associated with Ciner is the use of tiny stones of many colors which give a shimmering effect to the jewelry.

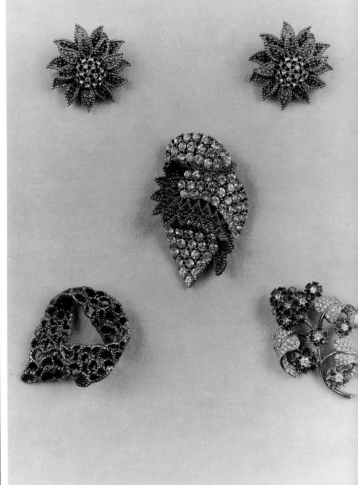

Group of three pins and a pair of earrings by Ciner.

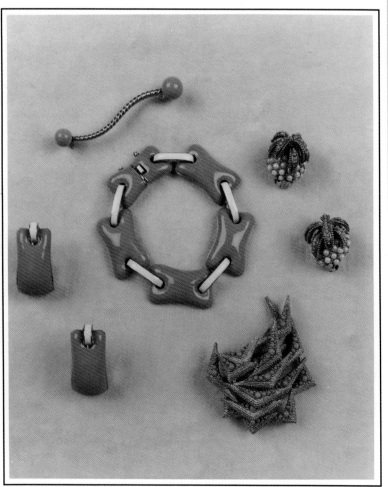

Turquoise-enameled bracelet, matching earrings and pin; pair of earrings with tiny turquoise stones and pearls; and pin of gold in granules and turquoise stones, all by Ciner.

Pair of bow-shaped earrings set with tiny pearls and red and blue stones by Ciner, circa 1959; pin with blue enameled leaves and many small pink and blue stones by Ciner, circa 1965; pair of floral earrings with small colored stones by Ciner, circa 1959; necklace of wirework with floral cluster clasp, French, circa 1948.

Opposite:
Necklace of turquoise and rhinestone-set links by Ciner, 1989.

Three bangle bracelets with figural themes made in the late 1980s: lion with green eyes and rhinestones by Ciner; panda of black and white enamel on golden bamboo style band; and zebra with green eyes, rhinestones and black enamel, unmarked.

Earrings and matching blue and green enameled circle pin by Ciner; large crescent pin with blue and green stones is unmarked; crescent pin with Buddah and pearl by Swoboda.

Elaborate fringe necklace of rhinestones and five large blue stones by Ciner, 1989.

Four pins of floral motifs made
by Ciner in the early 1960s.

Necklace of gold chain with
jeweled animal heads by Ciner,
late 1970s.

Necklace of black stones and gold links by Ciner, late 1970s.

Choker necklace of enamel and stone-set links in a neo-Renaissance design by Ciner in the late 1980s.

Choker of silver rope links and a stone-set cluster by Ciner, late 1980s.

Gold chain choker pave set with rhinestones
by Ciner, late 1980s.

Matching set of necklace, bracelet and
earrings carrying out a red, white and blue
color scheme in pave stones by Ciner, 1989.

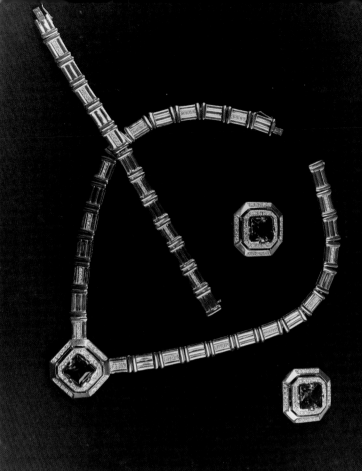

1980s

The decade of the 1980s continued the emphasis on sports, fitness and leisure time activities which began in the 1970s. Crushable fabrics requiring little care flourished in every style while sweat suits and tee shirts were worn almost everywhere. Women in the business world demanded classic and especially gold jewelry for the office. But the influences of glamorous women who wore fancy jewelry often, and a lot of it, such as Britain's Princess Diana, television star Joan Collins, music star Madonna and their like made dressing up both fun and fashionable once again.

In 1977, a synthetic gemstone named cubic zirconia which simulated diamond was perfected in Switzerland and by the 1980s its popularity in costume jewelry was secure. Sold under the trade name "Windsor Gems" in England, it has been used worldwide. Very large stones are possible in cubic zirconia which have remarkable brilliance at a fraction of the cost of diamonds.

When the Duchess of Windsor's jewels were sold at public auction in 1987, high prices were paid for them and imitations and like designs flooded the mass market which gobbled them up. Young girls enjoyed all the sparkling decorations of rhinestones in their hair, on coat lapels, ankles, wrists and fingers. By the end of the decade the market in both new and vintage costume jewelry was strong and growing.

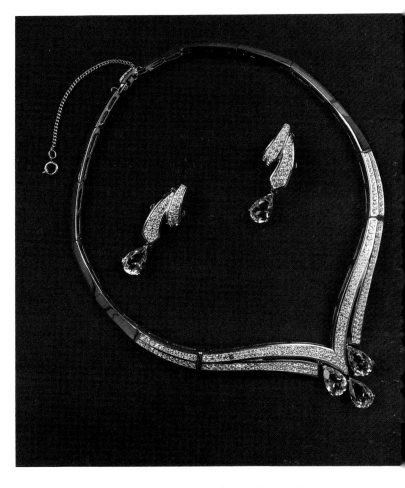

Necklace and matching pair of earrings of rhinestones with aqua tear-drop dangles, 1980s.

Opposite top:
Three necklaces and two pairs of earrings set with the brilliant synthetic stones of cubic zirconia, late 1980s.

Set of jewelry comprising a necklace, bracelet, and pair of earrings of gold-plated metal and rhinestone links and large emerald-cut stones, late 1980s.

Opposite bottom:
Matching necklace, earrings, and pin of English origin, 1985; and silk cord necklace of German origin, 1985.

Small stones of colored and clear glass have been carefully combined to create a single-strand necklace, a bracelet watch, a fine five-strand flexible choker, and a pair of earrings by Grosse for Christian Dior, 1980. Photograph courtesy of Fior.

Necklace and pair of earrings featuring a fancy bird head and ancient coin, late 1980s.

Necklace with blue stones framed by clear rhinestones and gold in this necklace of the late 1980s.

Burgundy-colored stones have been set in the links and pendant of this necklace from the late 1970s or early 1980s.

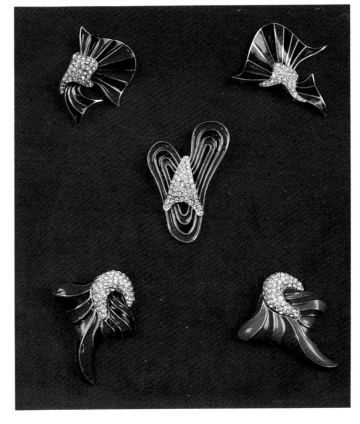

Five pins of blue and green enamel are accented with rhinestones.

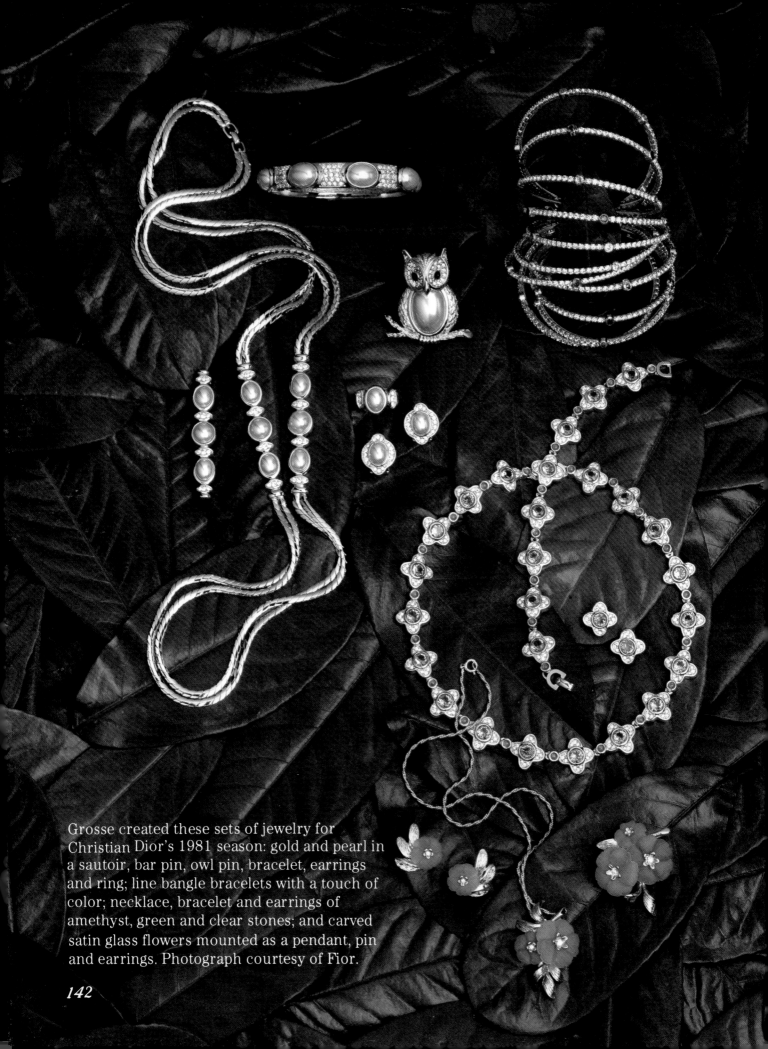

Grosse created these sets of jewelry for Christian Dior's 1981 season: gold and pearl in a sautoir, bar pin, owl pin, bracelet, earrings and ring; line bangle bracelets with a touch of color; necklace, bracelet and earrings of amethyst, green and clear stones; and carved satin glass flowers mounted as a pendant, pin and earrings. Photograph courtesy of Fior.

Pearls accented with colored pendants and matching earrings, 1981. Photograph courtesy of Fior.

Three sets of matching jewelry featuring red and clear stones with gold made in 1985. Photograph courtesy of Fior.

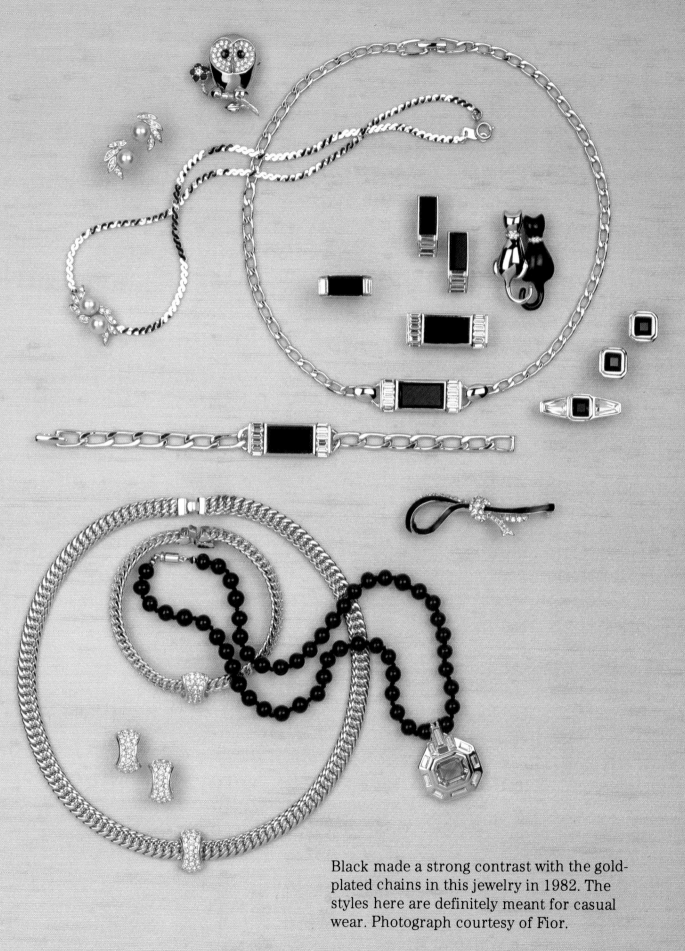

Black made a strong contrast with the gold-plated chains in this jewelry in 1982. The styles here are definitely meant for casual wear. Photograph courtesy of Fior.

145

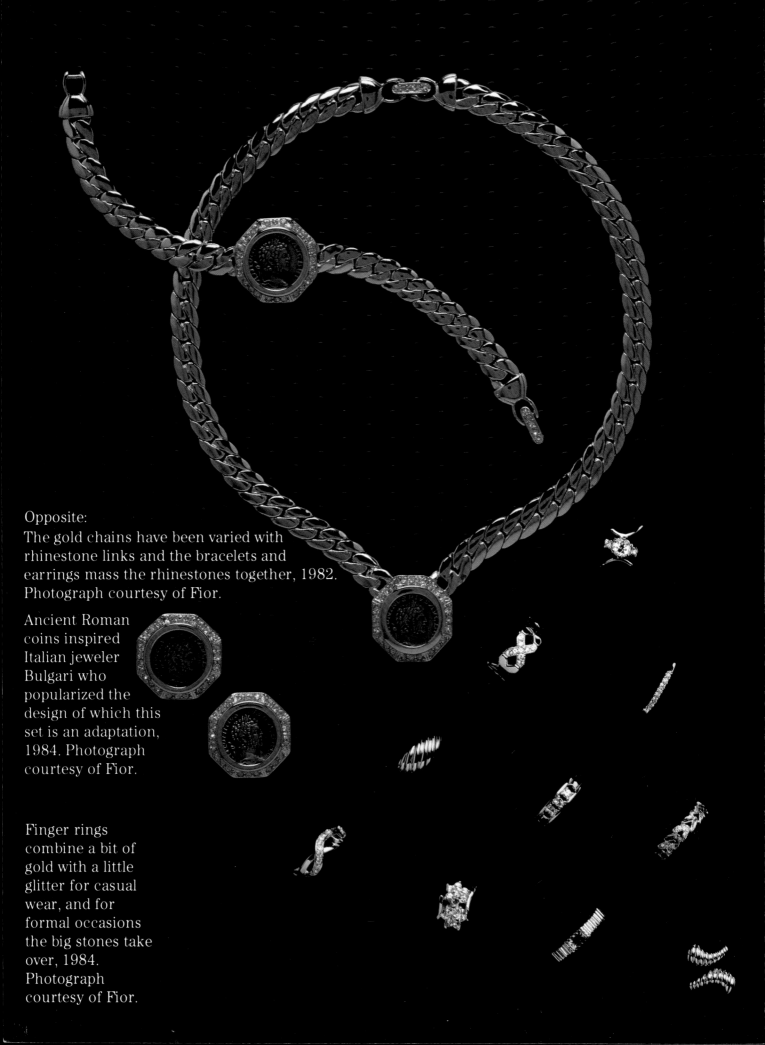

Opposite:
The gold chains have been varied with
rhinestone links and the bracelets and
earrings mass the rhinestones together, 1982.
Photograph courtesy of Fior.

Ancient Roman
coins inspired
Italian jeweler
Bulgari who
popularized the
design of which this
set is an adaptation,
1984. Photograph
courtesy of Fior.

Finger rings
combine a bit of
gold with a little
glitter for casual
wear, and for
formal occasions
the big stones take
over, 1984.
Photograph
courtesy of Fior.

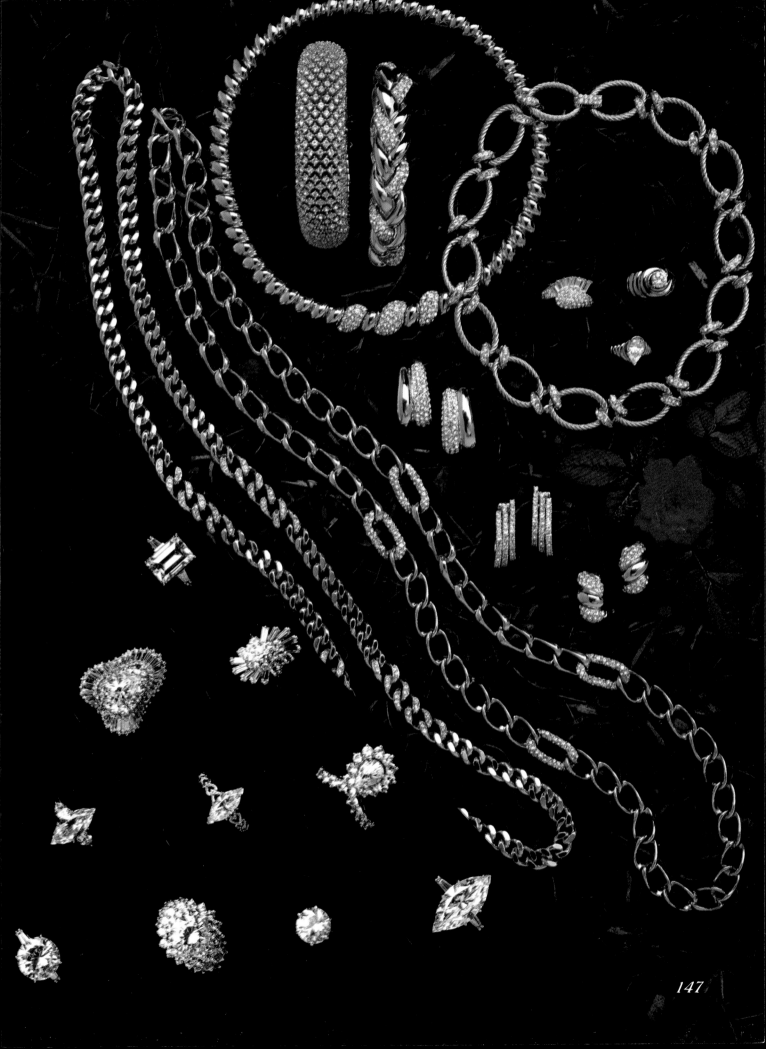

Animal heads form a theme with many variations in this jewelry from 1985. Photograph courtesy of Fior.

Red, white and blue stones are set in the links and pendant of this necklace from the late 1980s.

A return to the snake chains of the 1940s was seen in this set made in 1985. Photograph courtesy of Fior.

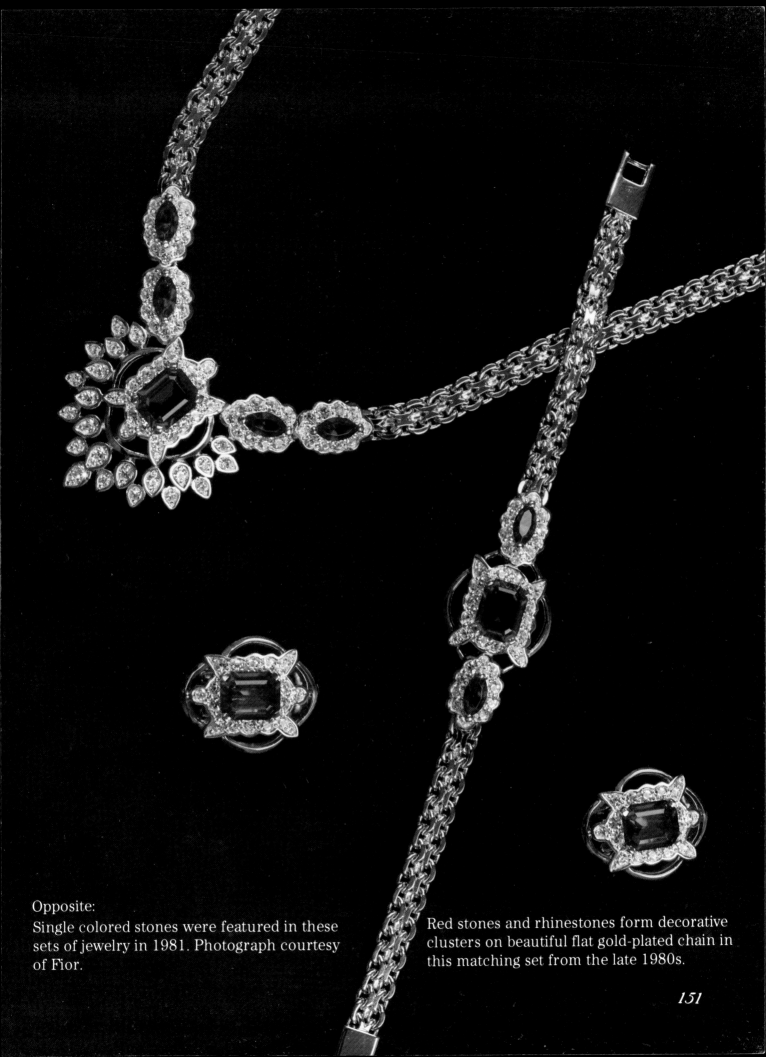

Opposite:
Single colored stones were featured in these sets of jewelry in 1981. Photograph courtesy of Fior.

Red stones and rhinestones form decorative clusters on beautiful flat gold-plated chain in this matching set from the late 1980s.

Beautiful gold work is accompanied by
colored stones and imaginative design in this
set of necklace, bracelet and earrings; and the
watch with lace-like settings, 1981.
Photograph courtesy of Fior.

The strong blue color of the massive stone is intensified by the line of clear marquise stones which support it in this nacklace, and the matching earrings complete the opulence of its design, 1988. Photograph courtesy of Fior.

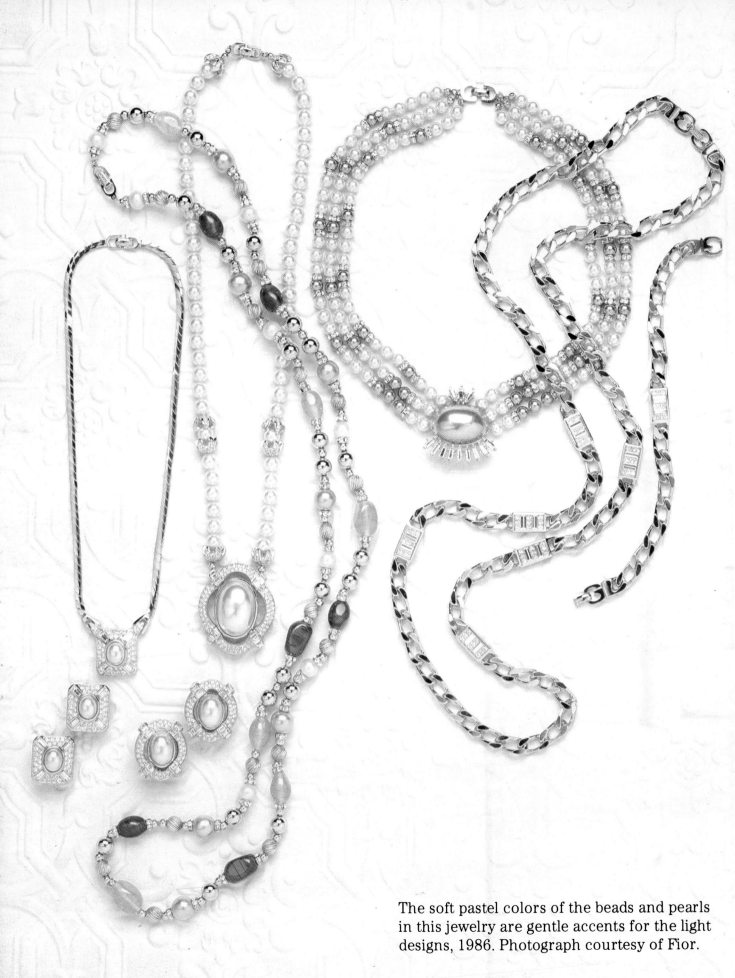

The soft pastel colors of the beads and pearls in this jewelry are gentle accents for the light designs, 1986. Photograph courtesy of Fior.

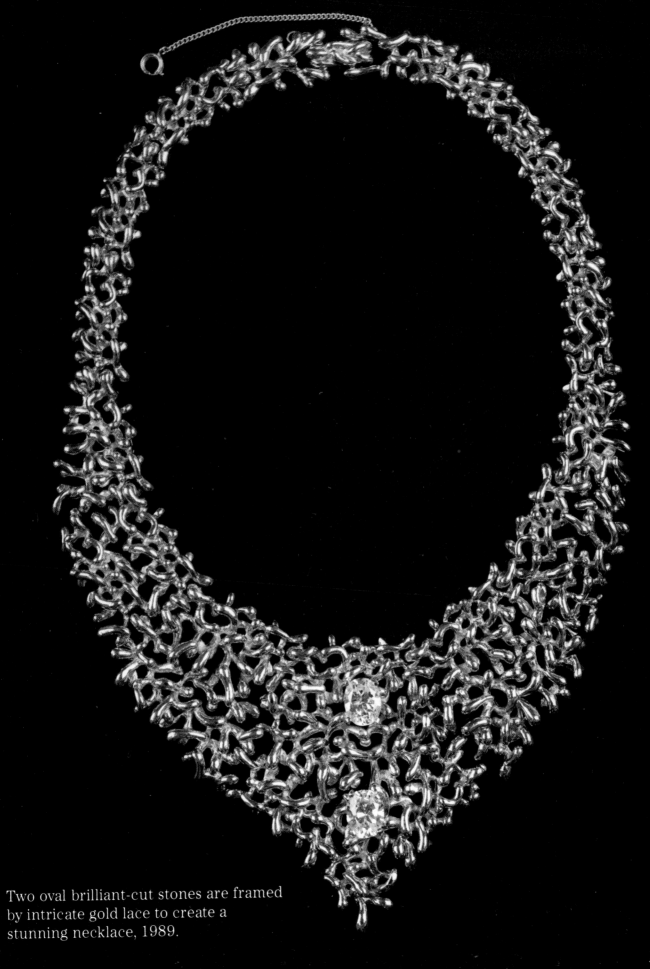

Two oval brilliant-cut stones are framed by intricate gold lace to create a stunning necklace, 1989.

Slick silver and gold accents carry out a
feeling of high-tech precision in this set of
matching jewelry, 1988. Photograph courtesy
of Fior.

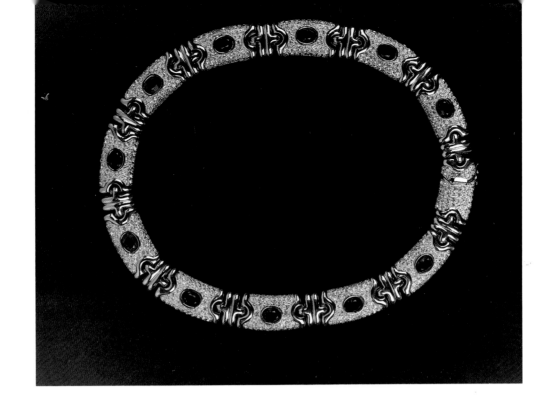

Necklace of pave links framing red and green stones.

Geometric lines and green stones break up the pave links of this collar, 1989.

Almond-shaped topaz stones are built up in framing rows of rhinestones on the links of this collar, 1989.

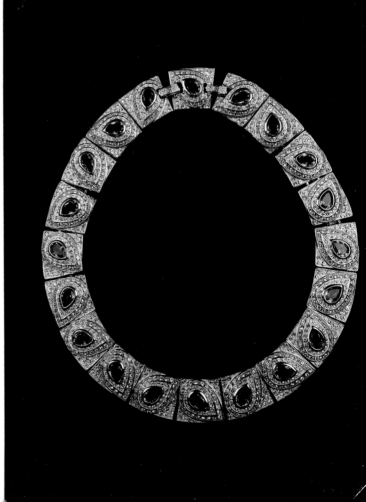

Necklace, bracelet, and pair of earrings with hexagonal pattern in black enamel and rhinestones, 1989.

Necklace, bracelet, and pair of earrings of pave gold links, 1989.

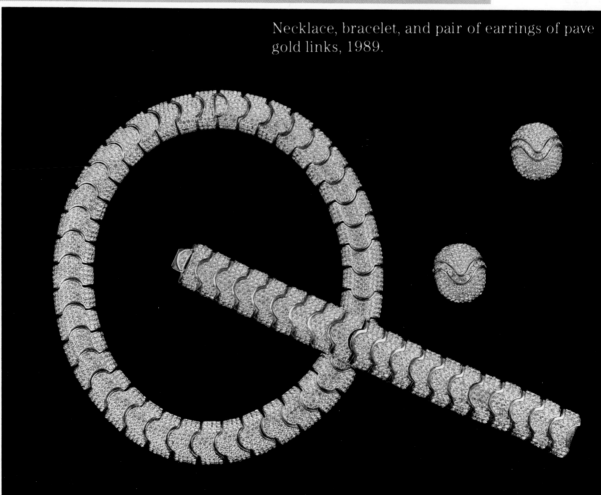

Aqua and clear stones make a pleasing contrast to the fluted gold links in this beautiful set, 1980s.

Aquamarine and clear stones entirely comprise the necklace, bracelet, and pair of earrings which seem to float because the setting is high and nearly invisible, late 1980s.

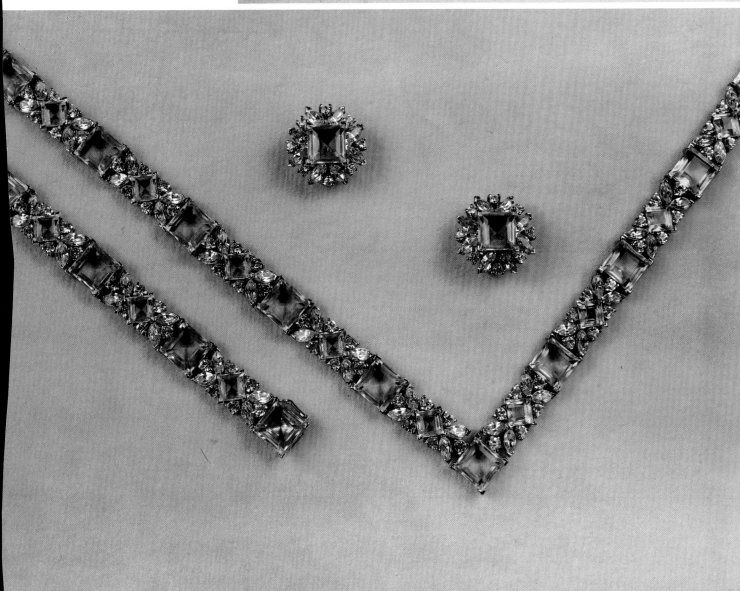

Index